Rise Up With Purpose

Transformational Leadership From The Inside Out

Dr. Michael T. Blue

THE BLUES PRINT GROUP

Copyright © 2025 by Dr. Michael T. Blue, DSL.

All rights reserved.

No portion of this book may be reproduced in any form without written permission from the publisher or author, except as permitted by U.S. copyright law. This publication is designed to provide accurate and authoritative information in regard to the subject matter covered.

Book Cover by Stephanie L. Blue

ISBN 979-8-9941120-0-7 | Paperback

ISBN 979-8-9941120-1-4 | E-Book

If you would like to purchase bulk copies of Rise Up With Purpose: Transformational Leadership From The Inside Out, please contact

The Blues Print Group LLC at info@thebluesprintco.com

Dedication

Nothing valuable has been developed without a sacrificial process attached to it. I am alive and well today with a sound mind, a strengthened heart and a renewed focus because of my Lord & Savior Jesus Christ. I believe that apart from Him I can do nothing and I am grateful for the grace he has extended me to document these thoughts with the intent of bringing light to someone who needs it.

To my wife Stephanie, who has displayed to me the sacrificial love and partnership that I will forever be grateful for. This would not have happened without your agreement and faith in the direction I believed God was taking us. Your encouragement when I was tired, your listening ear when I felt discouraged, and your kindness when I needed support made the difference in sustaining me throughout this process.

To our children, Olivia, Nicholas & Luke. Thank you for allowing me the space at our kitchen table or in the office with the computer to read, write, and grow. It's been a joy to see you all wait with patience and support me. Your encouragement has taught me how to be a better father.

To my Pastors Eric & Iris Butler thank you for believing in me, correcting me, and encouraging me to reach my potential. Your walks of faith inspire me and my family. We cherish every moment God gives us to serve, learn, and listen to your teachings about Him. We honor you both.

Contents

Introduction	1
Part I – The R.I.S.E. Framework	4
1. Why We Must Rise	5
How Did You Get Here Today?	
Transformation is a Process	
Transformational Stages	
Identifying the Transformational Leader	
Value of Transformational Leadership	
A Different Leader	
2. REFLECTION	18
Knowing Yourself Before Leading Others	
The Journey of Reflection	
Early Adversity	
Navigating Ambiguity	
Endurance	
3. INSPIRE	31
The Power of Vision & Story	
The Power of Story	
Early Beginnings	
Transformational Development	

    Mentoring a King

    Keys to Transformation

4. SERVE — 44

    Transformed to Take Flight

        Divine Timing

        Flight Phases

        A Pilot is Born

        The Cost of Transformation

        Questions to Ponder

5. ELEVATE — 55

    Multiplying Leadership Impact

        Photographic Memories

        Difficult Moments

        The Leaders Path

        New Beginnings

        Next Steps

PART II - Rising in Contexts — 67

6. R.I.S.E. in the Classroom: Leadership in the Classroom — 68

    Born to Fly

    Curiosity

    New Beginnings

7. R.I.S.E. in Business: Leadership Beyond Profit — 83

    Transformed For Purpose

    Let's Paint the Picture

    The Challenge of Transformation

    What is Your Story

    Equal Opportunity

8.	R.I.S.E. in Life and Community: Everyday Leadership	97
	Fear	
	Open My Eyes	
	From Small Steps to Big Leaps	
	The Leaders GPS	

Part III – Your Rise — 109

9. **The Commitment to Rise: Living the Framework** — 110
   - Challenging Beginnings
   - Will You Lead?
   - Fresh Vision
   - The Extra Mile
   - How To Function
   - Establishing Credibility
   - Transformational Journey

10. **Beyond The Climb** — 123
    - Leadership Is An Inside Job
    - How Do You See Yourself?
    - Be A Difference Maker
    - Take Ownership Of Your Story
    - Embrace The Ongoing Journey Of Transformation

11. **A Rising Generation: The Future of Leadership** — 132
    - A Life Transformed
    - Transformation in Practice
    - The Why of Transformation
    - Are You the Next Transformational Leader?

Appendix — 143

Introduction

You can feel it, can't you?

That quiet pressure beneath the surface.

That sense that you are meant for more than the life you're currently living.

That tension between who you are… and who you know you could become.

Maybe you feel confined by expectations, responsibilities, or routines that don't reflect your true identity. Perhaps you're overwhelmed by the weight of leading others while feeling lost within yourself. Or maybe you're simply tired, tired of pretending, tired of performing, tired of wondering why the life you envision feels just out of reach.

And yet, even in the middle of the confusion, something within you refuses to settle.

Something whispers: **Rise**.

I understand that feeling because I have lived it.

Before I became a leadership development professional, before I earned a doctorate in strategic leadership, before I coached executives, students, teams, and organizations, I was simply a young man wrestling with identity, purpose, and direction. At twenty-one, I found myself consuming multiple books on leadership, manhood, and personal growth, not because I was academically ambitious, but because I was desperate. I was searching for identity.

Searching for a blueprint. Searching for a way out of the confusion and into a life that felt meaningful.

Global exposure came early for me. Opportunities that should have felt exciting instead felt overwhelming. I had to face the uncomfortable truth: it's one thing to dream of influence, and another to become the kind of person capable of carrying it. I wanted to make a difference, but I was wrestling with systems around me, emotions within me, and spiritual battles that wouldn't let me ignore what was broken. And even as I grew, I watched individuals, leaders, and entire organizations struggle with the same thing:

Everyone wanted change.

No one wanted to look within.

Over the years, in conversations with thousands of people, students, educators, parents, executives, teams, pastors, and innovators, the pattern never changed. People weren't struggling because they lacked skill, talent, or opportunity.

They were struggling because they lacked alignment.

Who they were on the outside didn't match who they were on the inside.

And that disconnect was costing them:

Their confidence, their relationships, their vision, their joy, and their ability to lead.

This book was born out of that tension.

Rise With Purpose is not just a collection of ideas. It's grounded in the principles of transformational leadership, providing a distilled framework of transformed lives. A summation of the lessons, failures, breakthroughs, and truths that rebuilt me and so many others from the inside out. It is a blueprint designed to help you create the same transformation in your life, your family, your leadership, and your future.

INTRODUCTION

This book will challenge you to reflect deeply, inspire boldly, serve intentionally, and elevate courageously. It will push you to look inward before you lead outward. And it will show you that the potential you sense, the *more* you feel tugging at your soul, isn't just a fantasy. It's a calling.

You don't need more motivation.

You don't need another title.

You don't need permission.

You need alignment. You need clarity.

You need the courage to **Rise With Purpose.**

If you're ready to stop shrinking, stop settling, and step into the identity and impact you were created for, then keep reading.

Your **Rise** begins here.

Part I – The R.I.S.E. Framework

Chapter 1

Why We Must Rise

> "Success is not final. Failure is not fatal. It's the courage to continue that counts."
> Winston Churchill

MOVIES PROVIDE US WITH the opportunity to explore our imagination in a way unlike anything else. The screens with digital enhancements engage us visually, audibly, and emotionally. Whether we are in a theatre or in the comfort of our home, leveraging a streaming service these movies can captivate us, motivate us, and frustrate us all at the same time. I've pondered why something seemingly so trivial connects with us in such an intimate way. I believe the answer is multifaceted, but for the sake of our time together, I want us to consider this angle. Storytelling is a powerful tool. It has been considered a delivery system for key messaging across multiple aspects of life, including business, family, and education. Dale Carnegie once said, "The great truths of the world have often been couched in fascinating stories."[1] From the perspective of movies, some of these stories have been so riveting and influential that their creation demanded a sequel, and in other cases a trilogy. When George Lucas directed Star Wars: A New Hope in 1977, it began a wave of distinguished movies featuring unique and interesting characters the public wanted to learn more about. The pattern found in the success of these movies from the past lives on today, and some have attempted to refine and build upon it, leading to a select niche of movies called origin stories, most popularized in superhero movies. Seeing the confident, defiant Batman begin from a place of fear and low self-confidence gives us an emotional access point to something we aspire to see within ourselves. Whether in DC, Marvel, or any other universe, you can find your hero in each of them; each has a specific, unique origin story that positions them to fulfill a purpose higher than they originally anticipated.

How Did You Get Here Today?

Every Leader has an origin story. Each of us has, or will, experience a series of events that lead to a choice. The decision we face today is: what type of leader will we be? For those of you who do not believe this statement applies to you, allow me to provide some context. Currently, there are hundreds of definitions of leadership, which has led to much confusion in society. To think, one word could bring about so much division, but if harnessed correctly, it could produce clarity. The dichotomy in leadership is fascinating. So instead of giving you a long-drawn-out definition of what researchers believe leadership to be, let's acknowledge that, in its simplest form, leadership is influence. At one point in your life, did you express a level of influence? If you can identify those moments, you can also identify the expression of leadership within them.

Consider a child who cannot quite speak but has enough awareness to scream in a way that grabs their parents' attention so they can obtain a meal, be changed, or be held. In whatever capacity the child wanted to be supported, they took it upon themselves to influence others, which led to the fulfillment of that child's desire. Perhaps this example is too trivial. Think about the single mother who arranges summer activities for her children while managing her own work-from-home business and ensuring that every night her kids are seated at the table, with no digital devices, so they can dialogue about the day. This mother's expression of leadership is impacting her children and her community in ways that she may never understand or witness, but her influence is lasting. Or in corporate America, the high-performing individual contributor who does not believe they are ready for management responsibility provides counsel to fellow teammates, collaborates cross-functionally, challenges the status quo, and consistently develops processes that streamline workflows at scale. Would you consider this individual a leader? Unfortunately, some of us would not. So how do we shift this narrative about leadership? Our mindset about leadership needs to be transformed.

Transformation is a Process

There are many styles of leadership expression, from situational to behavioral, authentic to inclusive, and so much more. However, one of these leadership styles is so radical, so against the normality of life, that its impact has historically been revolutionary. Transformational leadership sounds like catchy corporate terminology but it is far from that. The purpose of this journey is not to define what good leadership looks like but rather to explore the need for transformation within each of us. Everything created has undergone some type of significant transformation before it has been purposed for use. Consider how a caterpillar, limited to a life of crawling, exposed to the elements and the dangers of life, has the innate ability and need to change into something more. That, in its final state, is a butterfly with the ability to view life from a different vantage point. No longer confined by its environment, it is open to the idea of something new.

Before we introduce what transformational leadership is, let's ensure we understand what it is not. As we will discuss, transformation alludes to action or movement, which gives us a major hint. No movement, no transformation. A leader who remains laissez-faire in their approach will never be transformational.

The process of transformation the caterpillar undergoes is called metamorphosis. The Merriam-Webster dictionary defines this as "a change of physical form, structure, or substance especially by supernatural means."[2] The process is viewed as supernatural because the change is something difficult to comprehend. One moment, the caterpillar enters a cocoon or a posture of stillness, and when the cocoon opens, a completely different creature emerges. The symbolism of this process is relevant to our lives. We all find ourselves in moments or seasons where life feels put on pause. The need to fast forward causes anxiety, and not seeing any change can be discouraging. However, the Bible reminds us in Ecclesiastes that "time and chance happen to them all."[3] This means your origin story could be today. The moment you recognize within yourself that you are meant for more, and that your expression cannot be confined by your current situation, is your beginning.

Transformational Stages

Metamorphosis occurs in four distinct stages: Egg, larva, pupa, and adult.[4] For our learning purposes, we interpret these stages as symbolic representations of human growth and development.

- Stage 1: Immobile Growth (Egg Stage) – This represents the early "baby stage" or season of stillness, dependence, and quiet formation. Growth is happening, but progress is not yet visible.

- Stage 2: Curious Consumption (Larva Stage) – Here, like an active child, movement increases, and curiosity expands. This is a time of exploration, gathering information, and consuming experiences that fuel development.

- Stage 3: Reflective Isolation (Pupa Stage) – Similar to adolescence, this stage symbolizes the internal struggle and transformation that occurs in isolation. It is a season of wrestling, re-evaluation, and deep identity formation.

- Stage 4: Convergence and Maturity (Adult Stage) – The adult stage represents the moment of emergence when clarity, purpose, and identity align. This is where everything learned in previous stages converges, allowing a person to rise into maturity and significance.

Now that we see how transformation shows up in our human development, let's review how this may appear in our leadership. If you are looking for another expression of leadership, you can skip these steps; however, if you are looking to make an impact, prepare yourself for some turbulence. The first phase of transformation can feel akin to stagnation. This is where the budding leader recognizes that what they have done up to this point is no longer sufficient for where they are supposed to be. There is an inner hunger to do and become more, but no blueprint, no roadmap, or insight into the steps required to reach the next phase. Many who have had the privilege of learning from an organization the basic principles of timeliness, teamwork, and discipline eventually desire some form of growth. This may vary based on the individual's career trajectory, ambition, or passion but the concept remains the same. I remember, as a teenager working at a local fish market, that learning to clean shrimp by hand became my daily project. Eventually, I had mastered the process and was typically cleaning over 500 shrimp and completing a number of other tasks each shift. The environment, coupled with my desire to grow, led me to learn how to cook the fish and serve customers. I had no idea what the future would hold, but these basic lessons would play a role in shaping my leadership foundation.

The second phase is when the leader steps into exploration. They begin to ask themselves and others questions to help identify who they need to become and how they will get there. While in this posture of curiosity, the leader begins to wrestle more profusely with the tension of yesterday and the idea of tomorrow. To the outside world, they seem off kilter and not the same, but the reality is, they are no longer the same. They have willingly entered a process of transformation that will leave them forever changed as individuals and qualify them to ignite transformation in others.

The following phase of transformation is isolation. This is the most challenging stage to function in, but the most critical. Often, leaders are surrounded by a lot of noise, and if they are unable to step away from the noise and identify their own authentic voice, they will function as an echo rather than an original. This will limit their transformational capabilities, as they have not truly undergone a stripping away of the old version of themselves to fully embrace the newness they desire. While in isolation, it is easy to feel misunderstood, undervalued, and underappreciated. Isolation provides a clear perspective, like a sniper who must remain still to see their target from afar.

The final phase of the leader's transformation reveals itself in the depths of the individual. The leader has a reservoir of character developed through many means. The result is a person who remains open to learning, ready to act, and prepared to function from their being.

Identifying the Transformational Leader

Early in my life, it was very difficult to identify transformational leaders around me and within myself because their expressions were not demanding, domineering, or aggressive. Instead, these leaders recognized that followers need a model to have faith of what they have not seen before. They need someone who embodies the principles of transformation and not just someone who speaks eloquently. Put simply, followers need leaders who not only talk the talk but walk the walk. What I didn't realize is that as a leader walks the walk in these stages of transformation, they are often misunderstood. A budding leader can be seen as a nuisance for carrying a different perspective, but that doesn't negate their ability to lead. I can already hear some of you, and I agree. The timing of a leader's release is important, and this is a rabbit hole we will dig into further throughout this book.

Imagine your vantage point on a situation varies from that of your leader. Responsible, discerning leadership understands the tension between disagreeing and committing and recognizes the importance of navigating it. As a budding leader, there may be several items related to a decision you are unaware of because you are not in the seat of leadership. Experience, insight, foresight, and other characteristics all play a role in shaping a leader's unique perspective. I have been on either side of this conundrum and found that being quick to listen and slow to speak is a word of caution and counsel. Often, the budding leader's purview is limited, and time and experience can fill in the gaps that information cannot. Our access to information as new leaders can add tremendous value in certain cases, but it does not supersede our level of influence or experience. Therefore, leadership development is imperative for leaders and should not be skipped to ensure sustainable success in the future.

Value of Transformational Leadership

> *Crisis does not sway the transformational leader; rather, it calls them to the forefront.*

As a leader, transformational leadership begins within yourself. I will revisit this concept several times throughout this book, as this point cannot be understated. Often, leaders are viewed as aspirational figures that we remember for their accomplishments. We celebrate their highs without a clear understanding of their lows. The procedure of leadership transformation, which feels surgical in moments, yields a patient ready for release. The work behind closed doors without any attention has been completed. Now, when this leader is placed in the forefront, they revere the opportunity and approach leadership soberly as a privilege, not a right.

As a follower, the value of a transformational leader cannot be quantified. These are the types of people we learn to trust through their example and their willingness to give us the space to experiment and grow.[5] These leaders can envision future possibilities while maintaining an appreciation of the past, so they can convey a clear blueprint of what good looks like.[5] Often, their primary concern is the betterment of others, not themselves. I believe that time reveals the leader, but others argue that the leader creates the time. Consider every transitional moment in American history when the environment was in turmoil. Transformational leaders, like Abraham Lincoln and Dr. Martin Luther King, arrived on the scene with a sense of vision and direction the nation needed..

Crisis does not sway the transformational leader; rather, it calls them to the forefront. Esther in the Bible, who underwent a transformation of her own to be suitable to serve as Queen for the King, found herself faced with a deep challenge. An opportunity to save the Jewish people required Esther to take a tremendous risk for a larger cause, and the lesson of leadership is found in the passage.

> *"And Mordecai told them to answer Esther, do not think in your heart that you will escape in the king's palace any more than any of the Jews. For if you remain completely silent at this time relief and deliverance will arise from another place, but you and your father's house will perish. Yet who knows whether you have come to the kingdom for such a time as this?"*[3]

There are several insights from this passage that we can take away and apply today as transformational leaders. Firstly, calamity and challenge as a leader are unavoidable wherever you are in life. Whether you're in the palace with the king or homeless on the streets, we all must stand up and stand strong as leaders with conviction if we want to be transformational individuals. Secondly, if we miss our window of action or influence as a leader, someone else will have the opportunity that we chose to forfeit, and we will have to live with the consequences of that choice. Lastly, there is a time for every transformational leader to make an impact. The chaos reveals a leader who has been prepared by circumstance far ahead of their moment of disclosure. The urgency of leader readiness is sobering, given the pace of change it creates. Time is changing. Mayberry suggests there is a leadership crisis that needs to be navigated at a time when the multigenerational workforce is both shattering barriers and creating silos, adding further complexity to the overall leadership puzzle.[6] The challenge in this environment is redefining what good leadership looks like. Titles and ranks are no longer the only triggers of what distinguishes a leader. Maxwell believes positional leadership is the lowest form of leadership and considers it entry- level.[7] These are the traditional bosses or authoritative figures who lead through fear and intimidation, and only achieve compliance through circumstance. The business landscape has become more complex with advances in technology. Organizations are still required to be both efficient and effective, and have done so by redistributing leadership authority, making structures flatter. The result is that many leaders now have to influence without authority by building relationships and listening to their peers' needs.

A Different Leader

The opportunity for a different type of leader has never been more evident. Consider Jack Welch, the former CEO of General Electric (GE). Known to many as the greatest CEO of the 21st century due to his efforts to increase the stock value and overall profitability of GE in his tenure. Specifically, he was known for his commitment to leadership development and for providing clear direction while offering actionable feedback.[8] From a transformational leadership perspective, Jack Welch's beliefs in a corporate setting were so impactful that many corporations globally implemented his practices, looking to replicate his success, which is an example of idealized influence. Or Pat Summit in the athletic arena. Her legacy is not limited to trophies, tournaments, or titles; it is the overwhelming impact she had on her teams. Pat would role-model the behaviors and character traits it took not only to be successful in her program but also to be a leader in life.[5] She leaned into individualized consideration through her ability to connect with each player separately on and off the court. She identified the strengths and limitations of each of her players through a series of tests and assessments, providing the context necessary to turn a group of leaders into a functioning team. Her persistence in constantly challenging them to exceed their own expectations demonstrated her ability to bring out the best in her teams. Her transformational leadership style was not soft but edgy, demanding that others become comfortable living outside their comfort zones.

I am sharing these insights with you not to discourage you but to give you a clear picture that sets your expectations. If you are reading this book, it is because you are curious enough to recognize that there is more. You understand that you are more than your circumstances and there is more for you to do. Leadership is a journey through turbulent waters, low valleys, and high mountaintops. Because of this reality, we are fortunate enough to glean from historic figures who have given us a blueprint for what transformational leadership looks like. The history of our nation has been layered with examples of endurance, creativity, and change. In the minority community, these stories of endurance have become calls to action and examples of hope for others. Throughout this book, we will investigate the lives of a number of minority leaders who transformed their generation and the impact they have had on us that we can feel today.

While these individuals have made a significant historical impact as leaders, their stories may be unknown to some. That is by design. Your legacy as a leader may not be visible in your generation, but that does not diminish the impact you will or can have. Minorities have often been in situations where they are the first to break through and have to represent more than themselves, without asking for the additional pressure that comes with the assignment. If you have ever been in a room where you felt ill-equipped, underqualified, or curious about how you can function effectively without appearing out of place, this book is for you. At the beginning of each chapter, we will look at historical quotes from transformational leaders that encapsulate themes found in our characters of study. At the end of each chapter, there will be a self-reflective assignment designed for you to further ingest the lessons gained from the lives of these leaders while exploring how this applies to you today. Remember, transformational leaders stand out. They have a unique confidence, shaped by their beliefs and values, that transcends race, sex, or socioeconomic status. Welcome to your journey of inner transformation.

---

1. Gallo, C. (2014). Talk Like Ted: The 9 Public-Speaking Secrets of the World's Top Minds. St. Martins Griffin.

2. Merriam-Webster. (n.d.). Metamorphosis. In *Merriam-Webster.com dictionary*. Retrieved from https://www.merriam-webster.com/dictionary/metamorphosis

3. The Holy Bible, New King James Version. (1982). Thomas, Nelson, Inc.

4. Marvelous Metamorphosis (n.d.). Natural History Museums of Los Angeles County. https://nhmlac.org/marvelous-metamorphosis

5. Kouzes, J.M., & Posner, B.Z. (2017). The Leadership Challenge 6th edition. John Wiley & Sons, Inc.

6. Mayberry, M. (2024). The Transformational Leader: How the world's best leaders build teams, inspire action, and achieve lasting success. John Wiley & Sons, Inc.

7. Maxwell, J.C. (2011). The 5 Levels of Leadership. Hachette Book Group.

8. Sosik, J.J., & Jung, D. (2018). Full Range Leadership Development. Routledge.

Chapter 2

REFLECTION

Knowing Yourself Before Leading Others

"Do not go where the path may lead, go instead where there is no path and leave a trail."

Ralph Waldo Emerson

EVERY TRANSFORMATIONAL JOURNEY DOES not begin with a title, position, or a team to lead, but with reflection. Before leaders inspire, serve, or elevate, they must look inward. Reflection is more than self-analysis; it is the act of aligning who you are with how you lead. In a world that prizes speed and visible results, reflection asks us to pause, consider our values, and answer the foundational question: Why do I lead? Leadership without reflection is like navigating without a compass or an activity without direction. The ability to pause, assess, and clarify values is what separates leaders who manage tasks from those who inspire transformation.

The Journey of Reflection

The beginning of any leadership journey always feels the most uncertain. Starting a family, building a career, or stepping into a new role is filled with questions and ambiguity. The road less traveled rarely has signposts. Yet, transformational leaders view uncertainty not as an obstacle but as an invitation.

Consider Alice Marie Coachman, the first black woman to win an Olympic gold medal and the first African American to earn an endorsement deal.[1] Her journey was not simply about athletic excellence; it was a classroom for growth, resilience, and purpose. As leadership author Samuel Chand reminds us, *"there is no growth without change, no change without loss, and no loss without pain."*[2] Alice's reflection allowed her to interpret hardship as preparation rather than punishment. Reflection turns pain into wisdom, setbacks into stepping stones, and confusion into clarity.

Early Adversity

Alice grew up in the segregated or Jim Crow South born in Georgia 1923.[1] She was one of ten children to Evelyn and Fred Coachman and was raised during a time of turmoil in our nation. Coming from a large family during a time when the economy was suffering, and segregation was commonplace, Alice found herself leaning into her athletic ability and curiosity to quench her passion to be more than her current circumstances allowed her to see. Her outlet from her set of conditions was running. Alice didn't run as a means of escape but as a means of access. She was purposeful in her athletic pursuits, and even when she was denied access to regular training facilities and did not have her parents' full support, she improvised. Her imagination saw the dirt roads of the south as a track, and sticks became hurdles.[3] Before being given the opportunity to compete against other children, her persistence and discipline gave her a mental edge. Alice ran barefoot and gained the additional support of her fifth-grade teacher, Cora Bailey, and her aunt Carrie Spry, who continued to develop and nurture her talents. Eventually, her work ethic garnered the attention of Tuskegee Institute, which offered her a high school scholarship at the age of sixteen. Her parents, who initially opposed a young lady pursuing the dream of running professionally, adjusted their perspective and aligned with their daughter's aspiration. Because she was in a segregated South, she competed on and against all black teams, dominating Amateur Athlete Union (AAU) competitions. She then enrolled at the collegiate level at Albany State College, where she became the national champion in the 50- and 100-meter races, the 400-meter relay, and the high jump. She was a world-class athlete who needed a world stage to display her talent. Unfortunately, while she was perhaps at the peak of her athletic prime, she would have to wait to compete on a global stage as the next two Olympic Games of 1940 and 44 were cancelled due to World War II.

Can you see the amount of adversity Alice faced in the early part of her life? While segregation may not be as openly accepted as it was in our nation during this time, prejudice, war, and confusion surround us all today, no matter the color of your skin or social class. Many of you reading this have dreams and aspirations that keep you up at night. Some of you have taken steps beyond simply writing down your vision and have begun the necessary preparation for your moment. You can empathize with Alice. Filled with potential and no outlet. For the transformational leader inside you, this is the moment when you recognize there is more for you, but the price of the process feels overwhelming. Clinton describes this as the obedience check for the emergent leader.[4] Essentially, when obedience is logical and necessary, our finite understanding of the greater picture does not matter as much as it does when we are clueless about what's to come.

Navigating Ambiguity

In The Matrix, a scene shows the machines on the verge of entering an underground city called Zion, where all the humans have been hiding and preparing for war. The General is speaking with the high council, explaining to them his strategy to defend the city and the preparations that have been put in place. A member of the council suggests that he allow one of his ships and captains to be sent out to obtain word on the whereabouts of the main character of the franchise, Neo. The General disagrees with the request and expresses his discontent, noting that he does not understand why the counsel would make such a ridiculous request. The response from one of the counsel representatives is a lesson that transformational leaders can gain much insight from. *"Comprehension is not a prerequisite for cooperation."* Let this statement sink in a bit. If you believe, as a leader, that every scenario, circumstance, or person can be put into a category and handled accordingly without nuance, you are mistaken. Situations arise in the life of a leader that require them to be agile and flexible enough to go with the flow or break the status quo at any given moment. Ambiguity is the transformational leader's partner as they learn to navigate the terrain in different seasons of life.

Alice eventually had the opportunity to fulfill her dream of representing the USA at the 1948 Olympic Games in London, where she set a new Olympic record and won a gold medal in the high jump.[5] King George VI, the father of Queen Elizabeth II, awarded her this honor. Alice began a life filled with small beginnings of segregation, poverty, and despair, and ended up being issued an

Olympic gold medal by royalty. Her transformational life did not stop there; she would go on to become the first African American spokesperson for Coca-Cola, with an endorsement deal in 1952. In her later years, she founded the Alice Coachman Track & Field Foundation to help support younger athletes and assist retired Olympians. Alice embodied transformation throughout her entire life. One of the characteristics of a transformational leader is their ability to inspire followers toward a shared vision. Alice, while walking on her road toward success, raised the bar beyond her circumstances. Her path was not straight, and there were plenty of moments throughout her life when she let her pain push her to greatness. So, as an older woman, when she spoke to the next generation, preparing them for the pressures of athletics and life, her words felt different in a tangible way. One of my mentors once told me, "A man with an experience will never be at the mercy of a man with an opinion." Isn't it interesting that hearing the perspective of someone who experienced hardship is more compelling than hearing the ideas of someone with ideas? Our natural inclination to follow is based on someone who establishes credibility with us. Kouzes & Posner found in their research that credibility is truly the foundation of leadership.[6] So, what does this have to do with being a transformational leader? EVERYTHING!

Endurance

> *Leaders will fail.*

Dr. Henry Cloud suggests that when a transformational leader is in place, the organization's identity changes.[7] They empower individuals to fully engage in their work, which builds momentum that leads to adaptation and learning, yielding growth in people and forward motion. Let's break that down. When someone's identity changes, everything about them changes. How they speak, look, function, and how you perceive them. Transformation is about change, and these leaders shake up the distinguishing characteristics of people and organizations into something new. This newness then leads to results that were previously unattainable and are now within reach. Execution enhances, and the focus of followers becomes more stringent. But the goal of the transformational leader is legacy.

Sustainable change is comprehensive and all-encompassing causing the leader to dig deeper than the surface level for solutions to challenges. These leaders identify root causes and are willing to perform surgery rather than place a band-aid on issues. How do they do this? They are lifelong learners. They display a hunger to grow that is infectious to those around them, causing others to desire to grow as well. The lessons they learn today to make tomorrow successful become a priority for them. Let me insert here that leaders will fail. Leaders will make mistakes, but the key is their willingness to take ownership of those errors and learn from them. Transformational leaders recognize that change is constant and that learning must be an iterative process they are willing to engage in. This passion for learning fuels people's growth. Individuals who are in near proximity to a transformational leader by association are learners dedicated to their own growth. How do we know this? Transformational leaders are purposeful with their actions and time so we can deduce they don't waste too much of it. If you are near a transformational leader, they move to a different clock. The same twenty-four hours seem to mean more to them, as they often do more with less. Learning, adaptation, and growth culminate in forward motion.[6] These organizations and individuals are not stagnant, but they identify opportunities others do not see, and they act. They are less risk-averse because they have tried and failed more quickly in the past, which gives them the confidence to try new things.

Alice is no different than you and me, so much so that after her illustrious career climaxed with the winning of the 1948 gold medal in the Olympic Games, she retired. She was a woman of great focus and determination and would later tell her children and others, "Guts and determination will get you through."[1] Alice recognized that life was challenging, and she was fortunate to have accomplished what she had so far. But she also embraced the discipline a transformational leader needs when facing opposition. Alice endured whippings from her father while she was a child, every time she went to practice running and jumping, because the expectation in her household was for ladies to be dainty, get married early, and raise a family. While eventually Alice would find herself with a family of her own, she did not allow perception or expectation to influence her decision to become what she believed she would be.

If we are honest with ourselves, think about how many times we have allowed others' expectations of us to dictate our choices. It happens all the time. Parents who desire for their children to become doctors, lawyers, or professional athletes when the child has a gift and a hunger for teaching. Or the young person impacted by social influence and peer pressure, so instead of pursuing their dream, which requires some additional learning, whether through certifications, bootcamps, or advanced education, they choose to start a business without the acumen for success and forfeit years of their lives trying to put the pieces back together. The life of Alice Chapman is a microcosm of this reality. Transformation is an inward process that eventually is expressed outwardly. Who you are internally will be seen externally. Or as the good book says, "as a man thinketh, so is he."[8] Who do you believe you are today? The interesting thought about your answer is that you still have time to adjust who you are tomorrow through your decisions today. While we have looked at Alice's life and seen our story in certain parts of it, I want to explore some key principles from her life that transformational leaders today need to consider.

Principle #1 – How can tomorrow be better than today?

As a young girl, Alice wrestled with the potential of tomorrow and the reality of today. Similarly, transformational leaders will find themselves navigating the same tension between what is and what could be. There are many differences between managers and leaders, and research has given us plenty examples. Managers tend to focus on process, while leaders focus on purpose.[9] Managers see systems and boundaries, while leaders envision potential beyond barriers. While the two are different, the actions and characteristics of each are critical for success. Allender suggests leaders are consistently torn between honoring what is good and true about today while remaining discontent with it in light of what could transpire tomorrow.[10] This is not a simple adjustment but a necessary one. The transformational leader must believe in the vision for tomorrow so strongly that the opposition of today fuels them in the process. Eventually, they begin to see opposition as a purposeful part of the journey towards fulfillment. The drive from that type of leader to remain consistent when being misunderstood is influential. Whether that individual was looking to be a leader or not, their actions and demeanor model the courage others desire to have and admire in their leaders.

Principle #2 – High expectations are normal

Alice saw winning as a necessity, but did not overlook the process required for her to be great. Her abilities were not limited to track and field; her speed was an asset she leveraged in other sports as well. While at Tuskegee Institute, she helped the school win three basketball championships and was named to five

All-American teams, becoming the only African American to do so. The expectations that she had of herself were always high and transferred to others she interacted with. Northouse suggests that a transformational leader's behavior will be exemplified by their ability to articulate goals, express confidence, and embody high expectations.[11] While more traditional models of leadership depend on external rewards, activities, or punishments, transformational leadership is about establishing the inner drive that true transformation comes from. Mayberry notes in his book that one universal principle of transformational leaders is that they commit to excellence because mediocrity isn't an option.[12] Some of us face very challenging circumstances that, in many cases, seem insurmountable. What is the difference between the individuals who overcome adversity and others? EXPECTATION. When we remove the option of failure from the equation, the only thing left is winning. This does not mean that, in the process, I will not fail; rather, I refuse to stay in a posture of failure. I will get past this trying moment because I understand I was created to accomplish more than my present circumstances reveal. As aspiring transformational leaders, we must remove the kickstand, stop leaning on our excuses for why we are not where we desire to be, and instead take ownership of what we can control. The mindset of a transformational leader sees opposition as an opportunity. Taking ownership looks like the opposite of the blame game. It is not pointing fingers or trying to identify the WHY; instead, it is curious about exploring the HOW. How do I balance my life and devote my time and resources to the right areas that will yield me the results I am looking for?

Principle #3 – It's not about how you start but how you finish

Alice Chapman died at 90 after a very fulfilling life. She embraced her childhood as a time when her surroundings could shape her without limiting her. As she grew, she realized her athletic potential would accelerate life opportunities for her. She capitalized on these moments throughout her life with discipline, dedication, and passion. Her life in many ways symbolized a race. Placed in the starting blocks in a staggered alignment, with the advantage lanes being given to others. Her discernment to realize this race would require her to be well stretched by life's challenges, which gave her the flexibility needed to accelerate when necessary. The beginning of her personal athletic journey on the backroads of Georgia, running barefoot, culminated in receiving a gold medal from a King. Transformation never ends the way it begins. An Eagle in its old age faces a decision: either die or undergo a painful transformation to extend its life by 30 additional years. A new beak and new talons used to capture prey require a painful rebirth, but for those willing to continue their race, they do it. Similar to you and me. Life begins, and the race has us in a particular category or lane that we can choose to change. I agree it may be difficult and require sacrifice, but when we remove our own excuses, we begin our journey towards becoming a transformational leader.

Reflection In Practice

Reflection is not a detour on the leadership path; it's the path itself. It grounds us in authenticity, steadies us in adversity, and prepares us for the influence we will carry into others' lives. To ***Reflect*** is to know yourself before leading others, and it is the first pillar of the **R.I.S.E.** framework. Before you move on to ***Inspire***, ***Serve***, and ***Elevate***, pause. Ask yourself: What truth about myself do I need to embrace today in order to lead with clarity tomorrow?

Reflection requires leaders to ask themselves hard but necessary questions:

- What do I believe?

- What values guide my decisions when pressure mounts?

- Who am I when no one is watching?

The answers form a foundation for authentic leadership. Without this foundation, leaders risk chasing titles or approval without knowing their true direction. With it, leaders build credibility that endures. Reflection also helps leaders confront blind spots. Without self-awareness, leaders may unintentionally create environments of confusion or distrust. But when leaders own their weaknesses and learn from feedback, they model humility and growth. Reflection doesn't make leaders perfect; it makes them real.

Reflection as a Compass

In my own leadership journey, I discovered that reflection is often the difference between reaction and response. When I took time to pause and ask, "What's my why in this moment?" I was less likely to react defensively and more likely to lead constructively. The same holds true for organizations: teams thrive when leaders know themselves and lead with clarity of purpose.

RISE IN ACTION

- **Values Inventory** - Write down your top five values. Which ones guide your daily decisions? Which needs to be re-centered?

- **Leadership Mirror** - Ask three trusted individuals, "*What's one word that describes me at my best?*" Compare their answers with your self-perception.

- **Personal Journal Prompt**: *What do I stand for, and how do my actions show it?*

1. Alice Coachman (n.d.). Biography. https://www.biography.com/athlete/alice-coachman

2. Chand, S.R. (2015). Leadership Pain: The Classroom for Growth. Thomas Nelson, Inc.

3. Essington, A. (1923-2014), Blackpast.org, March 8, 2009, https://www.blackpast.org/african-american-history/coachman-alice-marie-1923/

4. Clinton, J.R. (2012). The Making of a Leader 2nd edition: Recognizing the lessons and stages of leadership development. Tyndale House Publishers, Inc.

5. Boyd, H. (2014). Alice Coachman, an immortal Olympian. New York Amsterdam News.

6. Kouzes, J.M., & Posner, B.Z. (2011). Credibility: How leaders gain and lose it why people demand it. John Wiley & Sons, Inc.

7. Cloud, H. (2020). Boundaries for Leaders. HarperCollins Publishers.

8. The Holy Bible, New King James Version. (1982). Thomas, Nelson, Inc.

9. Zaleznik, A. (2004). Manager and Leaders: Are They Different? Harvard Business Review.

10. Allender, D.B. (2006). Leading With a Limp. Waterbrook Press.

11. Northouse, P.G. (2021). Leadership Theory & Practice 9th edition. SAGE Publications, Inc.

12. Mayberry, M. (2024). The Transformational Leader: How the world's best leaders build teams, inspire action, and achieve lasting success. John Wiley & Sons, Inc.

CHAPTER 3

INSPIRE

The Power of Vision & Story

"Peace is not the absence of conflict, but the ability to cope with it".

Mahatma Gandhi

PEOPLE DON'T FOLLOW TITLES, they don't commit to spreadsheets, task lists, or organizational charts. People follow vision. They follow a belief. They follow leaders who can paint a picture of what could be and invite them into that story. To inspire is to light a spark in others, helping them see possibility in the face of uncertainty. Inspiration is not motivational hype; it's a steady conviction communicated through story, vision, and empathy. Leaders who inspire move their teams from compliance to commitment.

In the movie Hidden Figures, we are introduced to three women who each must navigate racial and societal conflict to make a difference. America is in the middle of a race to space with Russia and other countries, and the pressure on NASA to ensure young astronauts have a safe trip to and from outer space is playing out on the national stage. Tensions are flaring, attitudes are overbearing, and individuals are competing to maintain a sense of value. The black women highlighted in this story are not only managing the challenges that come with being the first black women to achieve what they are attempting, but they must also put food on the table. Their careers are critical for their daily sustainability. The title of the movie is very fitting, as it can make a significant impact, seemingly from behind the scenes, in many people's eyes. While Howard Thurman the man himself is a chief historical figure in the eyes of some, he too may be considered a hidden figure infamous for mentoring and inspiring Dr. Martin Luther King Jr. At this moment your either aware of this man and his life or this is the first time you have heard his name and your curiosity is peaked due to the individual he directly impacted with his life, teachings, and story.

The Power of Story

At the heart of inspiration is story. Story communicates values in a way statistics can't. Story connects head to heart, translating vision into something others can feel and act on. History is filled with examples of leaders who inspired movements not by issuing commands but by telling stories that resonated with people's deepest hopes. Dr. Martin Luther King Jr. spoke of a dream, while Nelson Mandela spoke of freedom, packaging these concepts in ways that were tangible. Their words carried more than facts; they carried their belief. In your own leadership journey inspiration may not require a global stage. It may mean encouraging a colleague who feels unseen, rallying a small team toward a shared goal, or reminding a child that their life has purpose. Either way, inspiration flourishes in the presence of conflict.

Conflict, by nature, is transformational, and Howard Thurman was no stranger to handling conflict. Kouzes & Posner believe that what may seem like brick walls to many are doors to a few looking for a new future and willing to display how badly they want it.[1] Howard Thurman was one of those few who saw the opportunity in every closed door or brick wall. He became a theologian, author, philosopher, educator, and civil rights leader. He was a man of great precision and extreme work ethic. His life exemplifies the transformative power of a life lived well.

Early Beginnings

The story of Howard's life begins for us in 1907, when a young boy who was accustomed to seeing his dad on a biweekly basis due to his work schedule suddenly loses his father to a deadly disease.[2] In that moment, the responsibility of being a boy shifted to that of being a man in Howard's mind. Unfortunately, the coming days would begin to shape Howard's mindset in a great way. Howard's mother was a devout Christian, and his father worked on a railroad crew laying tracks on the Florida East Coast Railroad from Jacksonville to Miami.[3] Little did he know that in the future, his life would become representative of one who also laid down tracks to transport another generation of leaders forward into fulfilling their purpose.

When Saul Thurman, Howard's father, died, he was considered a sinner in the eyes of the church. His belief system was not grounded in Christianity, but he was a good man who cared deeply for his family and provided and protected them. However, when the discussion turned to funeral arrangements, the pastor of their local church refused to conduct the ceremony because of

Saul's lack of commitment to Christ. This led a traveling evangelist to perform the ceremony himself. During the ceremony, the evangelist Sam Cromartie essentially preached to Howard's father about hell as an example of what happens to a life without Christ. Somehow, the human element of compassion was lost as a seven-year-old boy had just lost the most important male figure in his life during a critical time of his development.[2] Why is this significant in the life of Howard and for us as aspiring transformational leaders? This course of events led Howard to state that he would never want to be part of anything related to the church in his life as a man. It thrust him into a posture where he would find more solace and peace in nature than in any interactions with humans. The woods' dangerous strength gave Howard space to explore his innermost thoughts and process difficulties as they arose throughout his life.[3] The connection between him and nature would later prove to be a catalyst for the transformational life he would embody.[3]

Howard grew up in Daytona, Florida, in what we would consider the black part of town, as there was a clear demarcation or wall of separation between white life and black life during his childhood.[2] In Howards older years he attended Morehouse College in Atlanta. To understand where Howard's fervor for social justice came from, we must envision the racial backdrop in the South in the 1920s. Georgia was filled with racial brutality, lynchings, burnings, and all other types of cruel behavior against blacks. This environment, filled with conflict, would serve to underpin Howard's identity, as he would find purpose in his pain and that of his people.

Bass & Riggio suggest that transformational leadership can be taught and developed over time, but many of its effects are directly correlated with our upbringing.[4] For example, in a study, Avolio and Gibbons compared transactional and transformational leaders and found that among highly transformational executives, a standard of excellence was coupled with high levels of support in childhood.[5] This study was not specific to a two-parent home or a single-parent scenario, but the common environment they were all exposed to was one where it was safe to fail if they tried their best. A learning mindset was instilled in these individuals at a young age, which led to subsequent learning in adulthood. This debunks the frame of thinking that transformational leadership is a location you arrive at rather than a destination you are ever engaging in.

Transformational Development

The years Howard spent at Howard University were in themselves transformational. He met many individuals during his studies, but one stood out. Up to this point in Howard's life, he was what you and I would consider the smartest one in the room. Howard was an intellectual with the curiosity of a cat. When Howard met Dr. Cross, a professor from Morehouse, he had met his match. Someone who was fully confident in their own ability and more than willing to challenge Howard to become the best version of himself academically. Dr. Cross carried with him a certain mystique of confidence that both intrigued and upset Howard.[2] He managed his classes with a meticulousness that made you respect what he wanted to accomplish more than the traditional professor. You were not allowed to challenge or dismantle any academic argument if you were not prepared to offer a subsequent academic argument in its place. Dr. Cross was the type of person who challenged you to become a better you. Think about whether you have anyone who fits that description in your life. If you do so, appreciate them.

Howard would go on to attend seminary with a sureness of his vocation to provide spiritual leadership to his people. The combination of his training and willingness to learn climaxed in his appointment as chairman of a delegation of Afro-Americans sent on a pilgrimage to India, where they would partner with the Student Christian Movement of India, and he would have the opportunity to meet Gandhi himself.[6] In the realm of transformational leaders, Gandhi stands as a strong model of this leadership type in action. Sosik & Jung suggest the changes he helped produce in India laid the foundation for the civil rights movement.[7] Gandhi was a man of profound influence who recognized the symbol he had become to many, so he consistently highlighted his infallibility and shifted the focus from himself to the ideals he believed in. As Howard's time in India ended, he had not yet spoken with Gandhi, but, to his surprise, Gandhi was making it a priority to speak with him before he left. He had questions about the Afro-American experience, about lynching, segregation, voting, and so much more.[2]

The two had a three-hour window in their schedules, during which they would discuss many things. Gandhi acknowledged during that conversation that, if he were ever to come to America to speak, it would be for the sole purpose of providing insight into the racial troubles that existed. He also mentioned that he would not feel qualified to do so until he had been able to solve some of the lingering challenges within his own country first, but that the learnings he would gain from that experience, he would want to share with the world.[2] Howard asked Gandhi why he believed he was failing to lead his people from the hands of the British. It was this moment that would mark Howard's theology, philosophy, and overall approach to solving the social justice challenges he knew existed back home. Gandhi told him that the effectiveness of an ethical ideal such as nonviolence depends on everyone's willingness to embrace it, not just the leadership.[2] Howard ended their conversation with one more question whose answer would further affirm what was already happening inside of him. He asked Gandhi what the single largest challenge is to why Christianity is not spreading in India. Gandhi's response was not another religion, such as Hinduism or Buddhism, but rather the way Christianity was practiced in Western culture. This statement highlighted Howard's concern about the religion that he witnessed when his father passed away, and a few other experiences throughout his life where it appeared that a man-made version of Christianity was being spread that was not breathed upon by God, which showed many an inauthentic Christian experience. Howard's challenge was not only to introduce the strategy of non-violence but also to model authentic Christianity and provide this experience to those he encountered.

Mentoring a King

> *Transformation is messy, it's painful, and it's aggressive.*

Martin Luther King Jr. and Howard Thurman had a connection steeped in black Baptist tradition. King invited Thurman to speak at his first pulpit in Montgomery. While they did not spend a tremendous amount of time with one another, there was an occasion where King found himself stabbed at the age of twenty-nine after the bus boycott, and in the hospital. It was there that Howard visited him and cautioned him to take some additional time off to disconnect from the movement before he found himself lost in it.[3] King took heed to the sage advice of Howard, and he was known to draw from Howard's teachings in several of his sermons in the 50's and 60's. Additionally, King adopted the discipline of non-violence through the insights of self-examination, meditation, and prayer he learned from Thurman. It was said that King held a copy of one of Thurman's books (Jesus and the Disinherited) in his pockets throughout the movement.[2] While Howard was not an activist, he was a catalyst to the civil rights movement through his teaching and counsel. The model for how spiritual and social transformation can work together is on display in the relationship of King and Thurman.

The word weakness carries with it the connotation of inadequate, not enough, and ill-equipped. The paradox of the transformational leader is that they influence and, in many cases, direct others, yet they cannot do so alone. The transformational leader is in a reciprocal relationship with their followers. They need people to be successful. The definition of success here will vary depending on what you're looking for. Typically, transformational leaders are in it for the long haul. They understand the value of today and delicately balance that with the extreme importance of tomorrow. Self-awareness of our own weaknesses as leaders enables us to empathize with those we influence. Recognition is key for the transformational leader, as they are concerned with the full human person being transformed.[8] For someone to be willing to extend themselves beyond their comfort zone for someone else, there must be a deeper-than-surface-level connection. The type of connection I am alluding to requires a level of transparency that some may consider a weakness.

Imagine the pressure we place on leaders with these unspoken expectations we have of them. We witness their success and influence, which translates into a perfectionist mindset. We place leaders of all arenas of life on such high pedestals that when they fall, they keep falling. How can we carry these expectations of others and not be willing to hold ourselves to the same standard? I am not suggesting we lower the bar for leaders who wield influence on function, but that we temper our expectations through identifying the right leaders to follow. Dr. Allender describes leadership as wearing a bullseye on your chest during hunting season.[9] It is not a simple task and carries the weight of responsibility like no other role. However, if a leader has not paid a price they can refer to, how can we expect any type of transformational experience from them? Transformation is messy, it's painful, and it's aggressive. There is no such thing as passive transformation; it is intentional and deliberate, and so is the leader's perspective once they have experienced a level of pain that has produced a transformational mindset.

Keys to Transformation

Charles Darwin is quoted as saying, *"It's not the strongest or most intelligent who will survive but those who can best manage change."* Transformational leaders are agile leaders. They are not limited to their own exposure but are willing to embrace the unfamiliar. Howard Thurman's ability to translate Gandhi's message of non-violence into a practical approach for leaders in the civil rights movement shows his willingness to break free from the monotony of sameness.[8] From his early childhood, he recognized that the church as he saw it could be more impactful, more influential, and more stable in times of trouble than others did, and because of his commitment to those ideals, many people's lives were changed.

Transformational leaders are lifelong learners. Their concern is becoming a better version of themselves daily, which internalizes their competitive nature. Instead of competing against people, they compete against themselves. Their validations come from their ability to block out external distractions and to leverage each day as an opportunity to change.[8] *What are they changing?* Their mindset, their outlook, their focus, you name it. They are not unstable in their thinking but purposeful in their approach, and if that requires flexibility with intent, they have enough courage to change course. As a leader, this may be one of the more challenging things to do. Acknowledge that what worked yesterday will not get you to where you need to be tomorrow, and make the adjustment. This is the messiness of transformation. It does not always appear linear, it's unpredictable, and it produces pain.

While transformational leadership is unpredictable, the leaders' value system is not. For this type of leader, values are an empowering factor that they leverage to empower followers.[10] Burns suggests *"the transformational dynamic that mutually empowers leaders and followers involves, as we have seen, wants and needs, motivation and creativity, conflict and power."*[10] Values strengthen leadership's impact and lengthen its reach as it mobilizes followers during conflict and competition.[10] Each of us has a specific set of values that we can articulate, or they are so ingrained into the fabric of who we are that they have just become an extension of our being.

Consider the leader who refuses to make decisions without a full evaluation. This type of leader values preparation and planning and considers them necessary for success. We all have innate values that undergird our decision-making. The transformational leader seeks to instill specific values in their followers that create lasting change beyond their time together. In many ways, we can consider the transformational leader selfless. Howard Thurman did not look to take credit for the impact Dr. King had on the world, but instead chose to fan the flame in the young activist while ensuring King did not lose his own identity as he navigated change and conflict. Transformational leaders place a larger emphasis on the specific needs of followers than other types of leadership.[11] The individualized consideration of these leaders manifests differently for each person. This may appear more instructive or, from a coaching perspective, more akin to situational leadership. The difference is that the leadership support given is more specific to the individual than to the circumstance. The focus is not on meeting the moment but on meeting the person and elevating them in a way that promotes longevity.

Inspiration in Practice

Inspiration often flows from authenticity. When leaders share their own struggles and triumphs, they give others permission to hope. Vulnerability, when rooted in conviction, becomes a powerful bridge. Practical inspiration requires three things:

- **Clarity of Vision** - Know where you're going.

- **Compelling Storytelling** - Share it in a way people understand and feel.

- **Consistent Action** - Support it with behavior that aligns with your words.

Without these prerequisites, our words will remain empty. With them, we will become leaders who spark momentum that carries us through challenges.

RISE in Action:

During my time as a leader, I have witnessed firsthand how inspiration transforms teams. When I shared not just what we needed to do but why it mattered by connecting tasks to the vision, people leaned in differently. Productivity increased, but more importantly, so did ownership. People weren't just executing a plan; they were participating in a purpose.

- **Craft Your Leadership Story** - Write a three-part narrative (Past - Present - Future). How has your journey shaped the vision you are inviting others into?

- **Vision Statement** - Draft a one-sentence vision for your leadership. Example: "I lead to help others discover their purpose and potential."

- **Influence Audit** - Identify one person this week you can inspire through encouragement or a story.

Inspiration is the bridge between reflection and action. Once you know yourself, you must help others see what is possible. Leaders who inspire ignite belief that transforms ordinary effort into extraordinary commitment. This is the second step in the ***R.I.S.E.*** framework: Reflect on who you are, then inspire others with your vision and story. In the next chapter, we'll explore what happens when leaders graduate from motivation to service.

---

1. Kouzes, J.M., & Posner, B.Z. (2010). The Truth About Leadership. John Wiley & Sons, Inc.

2. Thurman, H. (1979). With Head and Heart. A Harvest Book Harcourt Brace & Company.

3. Brown, L.C. (2023). What Makes You Come Alive. Broadleaf Books.

4. Bass, B.M., & Riggio, R.E. (2014). Transformational Leadership 2nd edition. Routledge.

5. Avolio, B.J., & Gibbons, T.C. (1988). Developing transformational leaders: A life span approach. Jossey-Bass.

6. Fluker, W.E. (2023). The Unfinished Search for Common Ground. Orbis Books.

7. Sosik, J.J., & Jung, D. (2018). Full Range Leadership Development. Routledge

8. Mayberry, M. (2024). The Transformational Leader: How the world's best leaders build teams, inspire action, and achieve lasting success. John Wiley & Sons, Inc

9. Allender, D.B. (2006). Leading With a Limp. Waterbrook Press.

10. Burns, J.M. (2003). Transforming Leadership. Grove Press.

11. Kouzes, J.M., & Posner, B.Z. (2017). The Leadership Challenge 6th edition. John Wiley & Sons, Inc.

CHAPTER 4

SERVE

Transformed to Take Flight

"The only limit to our realization of tomorrow will be our doubts of today."
                                                    Franklin D. Roosevelt

AT ITS CORE, LEADERSHIP is not about being in charge but about taking care of those in your charge. Titles and authority may open doors, but service sustains influence. To serve is not to lower oneself, but to elevate others by creating space for them to grow, thrive, and succeed. Serving as a leader requires humility, patience, and courage. It asks us to shift our mindset from *how do I succeed to how do we succeed together?* This change in posture changes leadership from transactional to transformational.

I have always been fascinated by planes and jets, and by how they maneuver in the air, where the possibilities seem endless.

From documentaries about wars fought with the US Air Force to movies highlighting the pressure pilots endure to sit in the cockpit, to getting on a plane for an overdue vacation with my family, flight symbolizes the opportunity to take advantage of it. What is most interesting about flight to me is aerodynamics. Simply put, aerodynamics is the science of how objects move through the air. The laws of flight are found in four principles necessary to sustain flying. These are lift, weight, thrust, and drag. Each of these forces is equally important and supports the others to achieve the goal of flight. Leaders who desire to be transformational all display the characteristics found in these principles. For the purposes of our learning, there is a historical model that embodies these principles not only in her character but also in her life.

Divine Timing

Bessie Coleman, the first African American woman aviator to earn a pilot's license, was born as the tenth of 13 children to her mother, Susan Coleman, on January 26th, 1982, in Atlanta, Texas.[1] She was a woman from small beginnings and limited opportunities. Her father realized that low wages and the endless cycle of limitation would be their lot if they opted to stay in Atlanta, so when Bessie was two years old, the family moved to Waxahachie, Texas where her father built them a three-room house instead of subjugating their family to the trap of sharecropping.[1] Bessie was born roughly thirty years after the abolition of slavery. She was in a nation where the idea of black freedom was still new and not widely accepted. Especially in the South, where laws were put into place and enforced by state legislatures, hindering African American progress at every turn. These laws were known as the Black Code. Liberty had come to blacks through the Emancipation Proclamation, but many of them found themselves in a hostile environment, undereducated and cut off from any semblance of normalcy, all by design.

Imagine for a moment it being against the law for you to speak to someone of another race without being spoken to, or it being illegal for a negro to be taught to read or write, own a house, own a gun, vote, or be outside after sunset. The list of ridiculous laws was endless. This is the time when Bessie Coleman was born. Jim Crow was at its peak, and it was precisely this environment that would produce in Bessie the fortitude to become a world changer.[2] Her father, George, attempted to convince her mother, Susan, to move the family to Oklahoma, where blacks were treated better. However, Susan did not want to raise her family in an environment with Indian customs, so she declined George's plea. The result was that George left Susan and the family to fend for themselves.[1] As if the odds were not already stacked against Bessie, but now the adversity had only increased.

Bessie would grow to enjoy reading and math and was heavily influenced by the writings of WEB Dubois and the life of Harriet Tubman. These figures became the heroes who gave her the imagination to believe beyond her circumstances. But the book *"Uncle Tom's Cabin"* was by far one of her favorite books. She would often read it aloud to her family and act out some of the stories, which may have given her a set of guidelines to live by. She would often tell her mother that she would never be an Uncle Tom, and she grew up with an attitude. She wasn't a woman who was accustomed to putting her head down in front of the *"white man"*. Bessie had an inner drive to go against the grain and swim upstream. Like the principles of flight, Bessie would, throughout her life, identify opportunities where she needed weight, drag, or thrust and lift to accomplish her goals.

Flight Phases

Transformational leaders operate outside traditional leadership guidelines. These are people who color outside the lines and always see situations or people through the lens of what could be, not what is. For a plane to fly, it needs to have a certain weight. Consider the weight we carry throughout life. I am not only referring to the physical weight in our bodies, but also the additional weight we carry. The burdens you bear, the stress you endure, the challenges you solve. All these areas of life, whether spiritual, emotional, physical, or otherwise, carry a weight that is necessary in the grand scheme of taking flight. Next time you're considering throwing in the towel because the pressure is too much, give thought to the idea that this could be part of your preparation for flight. There is a process for every promise.

Secondly, the transformational leader needs to drag for optimal flight. Drag can be interpreted as the resistance between you and your goal. When an aircraft is accelerating the drag reveals itself as an opposing force going in the complete opposite direction of the aircrafts motion.[3] If this doesn't make you think, I don't know what will. When I learned this principle, it changed my perspective on opposition. Instead of complaining about the opposition, I can now see it as a leading indicator that I am heading in the right direction. As we will see in Bessie Coleman's life, she had plenty of opportunities to turn back from pursuing her dream due to the staunch resistance she faced as a woman, as a minority, and as someone playing in a sandbox that was traditionally men-only. What opposition in your life is part of the drag necessary for you to get your wings?

The next phase of flight is thrust, which can be considered the driving force that moves the aircraft forward. This is what the engine is created for. The power to push forward at a faster rate than the resistance coming towards it. Bessie, the first African American woman pilot, would not only overcome the sexism, racism, and difficulties of her upbringing, but also become an iconic figure who would go on to influence an entire people. In America at that time, it was impossible for a black woman to obtain their aviation license and fly, but when she was speaking with her brother, who was a World War I veteran, he mentioned to her that French women were taking to the skies. Bessie interpreted this not only as a challenge but as a calling to something more. This led her to consult Robert Abbot, the publisher of the popular Black-owned newspaper, the Chicago Defender, about whether she should take the leap of faith to France. Robert would go on to advise Bessie to go because she would have a greater opportunity there and be more respected as a black woman.[1] Like her life, Bessie was always committed, dedicated, and willing to learn to get to where she needed to be.

Lastly, all aircrafts need lift to get off the ground or to a safe place and enter the unknown of the skies. Bessie witnessed her older siblings leave the small town of Waxahachie, Texas, with hopes of finding a better life in the north. News about Chicago, the second-largest city in America at the time, continued to appear in newspapers, promising a place filled with opportunity.[2] Eventually, the thought of stepping out of her comfort zone and trying something new would fuel Bessie to travel to Chicago as well. What she found was a place where Jim Crow laws didn't exist, but to gain access to the opportunities she dreamt of, she would have to be diligent. She would enroll in beauty school and take up manicuring as a profession. Despite this, Chicago would slowly see a rise in prejudicial acts highlighted by what history calls the Red Summer, which was a series of race-related riots. Fights, disagreements, and different values all reached a point where the Governor called the state militia into Bessie's neighborhood, leaving thirty-eight dead, five hundred thirty-seven injured, and more than one thousand people homeless.[2] These circumstances only increased her determination to go further than she had already come. She now had a blueprint of experiences to draw on, and her frame of reference for the impossible differed from many, which gave her the confidence to try what others would not.

A Pilot is Born

> *Transformational leaders see what does not currently exist.*

Kouzes & Posner believe resilient individuals are committed to forward movement regardless of the adversity they face because they have an intrinsic belief they can do something about their present situation.[4] In other words, they can influence the outcome of tomorrow by what they do today. Transformational leaders are those who unlock the full potential of their followers. They see what does not currently exist and instill belief in others by empowering them to become the best version of themselves. Mayberry informs us that inspiration triggers change and cannot be overstated.[5] Bessie's determination to realize her dream of flight would fuel her study of French while she sought other means of compensation to pay for her trip. When she had raised enough funds, she found herself on a steamship out of the country. Not to mention the hurdles she had to overcome to acquire a passport, this woman was resourceful, clever, and full of vision. Once in France, she would walk nine miles to and from aviation school every day for ten months.[1] Her dedication to her craft showed throughout her training period, as many other pilots in the program did not have the same amount of skill she possessed. Due to her dedication, she eventually earned an international pilot's license, which addressed the challenges she encountered in America.

In 1929, she returned to America to a host of reporters from all races wanting to gain access to her story, her journey, and her passion.[1] The transformational leader now had the opportunity to implement influence to change the course of history. A reporter once asked her why she started flying, and her response was that there must be African American Aviators, and that she felt a duty to show others the possibility of overcoming the impossible.[1] She would go on to open her own aviation school and lecture at African American theatres and schools with the intent of giving people a love for aviation.[2] She did many exhibitions, which established her credibility as a pilot and increased her popularity nationally. During one of her routine exhibitions, a wrench slipped into the control gears, causing the plane to nosedive. Bessie fell from the plane at roughly two thousand feet and was instantly deceased.[2]

The Cost of Transformation

Her legacy as a woman, influencer, pilot, leader, and seeker of truth was found in many places. She taught adults and children the passion of aviation and inspired many to become pilots, as over 10,000 individuals attended her funeral. Her skill as a pilot challenged tradition and fostered a fresh outlook on aviation. Her life can be encapsulated in a few words: don't be afraid to take risks, and let's fly. While Bessie lived a life meant for the skies, she embodied a transformational perspective that leaders need today. The challenges related to the economy, healthcare, socialism, and other issues have put leaders in difficult situations. For those who have been able to maintain a level of discipline and good character, the eyes on them are even larger as society looks to identify the kink in the armor or the flaw that would lead to a downfall.

The truth is, transformational leadership is not only something to aspire to but a need that meets the moment for today. Mayberry suggests that leadership is far from a straightforward journey.[5] It is filled with turns and pivots and requires a level of agility and resilience unlike any other time prior. Consider how the COVID-19 outbreak forever disrupted the world's rhythm, customs, and traditions.[5] We are in a period where transformational leadership will cost you something. Mayberry believes transformational leadership requires a selfless drive, unwavering dedication, and personal accountability.[5] Those words may either sound foreign to you or appear foreign in action in society. Consistency and self-accountability have not been qualities this generation has seen from its leaders. We have been exposed to scandal, lies, and false narratives to spin others into thinking what's right is wrong and what's wrong is right. When will the transformational leaders stand up?

Now, some of you may be wondering how I can make the type of impact that Bessie Coleman did? The answer is there will only be one Bessie Coleman, but the need for transformational leadership continues. Bessie chose to leverage her skillset to challenge and persuade others to a deeper understanding of their potential.[1] What her story tells us is that our external factors, and as challenging as they may appear, cannot stifle the willingness to pursue our dreams and become who we believe we were destined to be. In Bessie's life, she seemingly stumbled upon her purpose, but she was always in search of it. The transformational leader consistently seeks opportunities to influence others to become more than they are.

Questions to Ponder

What is hindering you from becoming a better version of yourself? Are you allowing yourself to be distracted so much by your present state that you find it challenging to envision your ideal state? I can tell you that I, too, have had to wrestle with certain restrictions or limitations that have prevented me from accomplishing certain things in certain seasons. I don't come from a wealthy background. I come from a middle-class family that, through blood, sweat, and tears, put a roof over my head, food in my belly, and clothes on my back. Were there moments where I felt my parents were socially absent, sure. Did this have an adverse impact on how I saw myself and how I saw life, absolutely. The transformational journey begins on the inside and is expressed outwardly. I remember reaching a point in my career when discussions about salary structure became increasingly uncomfortable for me. Not because I didn't appreciate being valued for my personal skill set, but because internally I struggled with whether I truly was worth my expectations. Generational mindsets had to break off me during my individual transformation, but this was not an overnight exercise. It was a continuous applied learning experience that took coaching, prayer, study, and forgiveness to overcome. Bessie saw similar challenges within her own community growing up in the middle of Jim Crow, but instead of turning a blind eye to it, she chose to act.

True transformational leadership requires sacrifice. It is a selfless responsibility where the best leaders are also the best learners.[6] Kouzes & Posner suggest that developing leadership expertise is a deliberate action that places a high demand on someone mentally.[6] The urgency to practice when no one is looking or to fine-tune your craft when you're tired, all with the hope and belief of being able to express this in a way that adds value to someone else in the future. The mindset of the transformational leader is not self-based. Therefore, when we see it in action, it appears foreign to us. These types of leaders are not only remembered for their accomplishments but more so for who they were. The personal character of Bessie Coleman provides a picture of the willingness to exceed expectations and to create an entirely new set of expectations for others. Ask yourself a question: Do you want to be remembered for what you have done or who you are? The answer to this will align your intentions, motives, and actions as a guiding light on the journey towards transformation.

Service in Practice

Practical service can take many forms:

- **Listening First** - Giving people the dignity of being heard before being directed.

- **Mentorship** - Intentionally developing future leaders by sharing wisdom and opportunities.

- **Sacrifice** - Choosing what benefits the group even when it costs you personally.

RISE in ACTION:

- **Service Audit** - List three people you influence. Write one tangible way you can serve each of them this week.

- **Listening Challenge** - For one day, commit to listening fully before responding. What do you notice?

- **Mentorship Path** - Identify one person you can mentor. Schedule a conversation to ask how you can support their growth.

When leaders serve, they redefine what success looks like. It's no longer about how high they can climb but how many they can bring with them. Service multiplies influence, strengthens culture, and sets the stage for the next pillar: *Elevate*.

Having reflected on who you are and inspired others with vision, the next step is to serve with humility. But transformational leadership doesn't stop there; it culminates in the ability to elevate others beyond yourself.

---

1. Hopson, C. (2021). A Pair of Wings. Jet Black Press.

2. Plantz, C. (2001). The Life of Bessie Coleman: First African American Woman Pilot. Enslow Publishers, Inc.

3. NASA, *Beginners Guide to Aeronautics*, "Four Forces," accessed November 3, 2025, https://www1.grc.nasa.gov/beginners-guide-to-aeronautics/four-forces.

4. Kouzes, J.M., & Posner, B.Z. (2017). The Leadership Challenge 6th edition. John Wiley & Sons, Inc.

5. Mayberry, M. (2024). The Transformational Leader: How the world's best leaders build teams, inspire action, and achieve lasting success. John Wiley & Sons, Inc.

6. Kouzes, J.M., & Posner, B.Z. (2010). The Truth About Leadership. John Wiley & Sons, Inc

Chapter 5

ELEVATE

Multiplying Leadership Impact

"Photography is the story I fail to put into words."
Destin Sparks

THE HIGHEST CALLING OF leadership is not what you achieve for yourself but what you empower others to achieve. Elevation is the practice of multiplying leadership impact by creating cultures, systems, and legacies that last beyond your tenure. A leader who elevates is not satisfied with personal success only. They measure effectiveness by collective growth. They ask not only "Did I rise?" but "Who rose because of me?" Elevation shifts the focus from the individual to the community. It fosters continuity, ensuring that leadership remains intact even when the leader exits. Leaders who intentionally elevate, develop successors, embed values in the culture, and design systems that outlast them. This is how leadership becomes legacy: by ensuring the work continues, grows, and evolves long after the leader has stepped aside.

One Sunday afternoon in my early twenties, I found myself in a movie theatre. I had snuck in with a group of my college peers to binge-watch the latest movies and eat popcorn until evening. As we entered the theatre through the back entrance for a showing, we were surprised by the action-packed previews and even more eager for the main event. The lights suddenly dimmed, and the environment hushed to the point where someone could be heard typing a text message on their smartphone. Within the first ten minutes of the film, a sobriety unlike anything I had ever felt before came over me. I positioned myself in a separate row away from my friends and engaged with the visual masterpiece. There were stories of records being broken by this film and of lives being deeply impacted as crowds around the world grew. Up until 2024, this was the highest-grossing R-rated film in the US. So many things were happening during this release, and I had no idea that my life would be forever changed by this experience. At the time, I was a struggling college student on the risk of academic probation for the second time and addicted to alcohol. Directly before the movie, my friends and I just finished smoking marijuana, and my eyes were bloodshot red as we entered the theatre.

The opening scene is a visual that will forever remain in my mind and heart as I witnessed it. The Passion of the Christ was a showpiece filled with drama, betrayal, victory, and pain. I experienced all those emotions and more as I sat sobbing in my chair and sobered up from what I was encountering. The impact of the images left a transformative print on me. Visual presentations have the power to capture and influence perception, unlike most things. The age-old adage that a picture is worth a thousand words takes on even deeper meaning when the picture touches you at your core. For the trained eye, these images depict a journey with stages that culminate in a final view. In many ways, the transformational leader's life reflects a similar journey. History bears witness to only a few individuals who encapsulate the creativity of a life of imagery, the way this man once did. Gordon Parks was a man at war with life his entire existence. Gordon did not grow up in an environment conducive to his success, so he needed to learn how to navigate the complexities of life with his weapon of choice, a camera.

Photographic Memories

The history of Gordon Parks cannot be told more appropriately than through the lens of a photograph filled with captivating moments that warrant being captured for history to observe the necessary lessons that growth produces when given the opportunity to reflect. The still images we will explore serve as a reminder of what was, what is, and what can be. Gordon's life began in Kansas, where he grew up exposed to segregation while in grade school. Whites and Blacks grew up with distinctive access to academic opportunities. Gordon was challenged by generational and cultural limitations from a young age. Kansas was the home of a young boy filled with segregation and murder. Imagine being only nine years old and considering yourself lucky to be alive as you witness close friends brutally beaten and shot.[1] Living a life filled with this type of emotional trauma at such a young age can influence someone greatly without a proper outlet or counsel. Such was the story of young Gordon.

In 1921, the Tulsa riots began in the surrounding states to Gordon's hometown.[1] He would hear stories of whites invading negro neighborhoods, resulting in all-out war on the streets. Despite all the negativity, including poverty, fear, and a host of other issues surrounding Gordon, the one piece in his life that brought a sense of stability and calm was his mother. She was a woman of the Methodist faith who instilled a love of learning in all her children, knowing they would need character and perseverance if they were ever to make something of themselves. Unfortunately for Gordon, his time with his mother would be short-lived as she passed away when he was only sixteen.[1] Gordon would have to face an unforgiving world without the comfort and direction of his mother and the lack of dedicated leadership from his father. Essentially, he would have to figure out life through trial and error.

This environment calloused Gordon's heart in such a way that it would lead to fits of anger and deep frustration even with his own ethnicity. There were instances as a young teenager where Gordon would question God's choice to make him a black man. He would dream of living as a white boy and envision what it would be like to not have to navigate the world with his set of challenges only to wake up with the realization that he was black and that was final.[1] Allender believes decisions become complex the moment that the past, present, and the future collide.[2] For Gordon, he would always find himself in situations where this was exactly the case. The concept of transformation alludes to becoming something different today than we were previously. The only path towards a transformational life is to boldly face all three areas with transparent courage, reaching a place of change.

Difficult Moments

The International Landscape Photographer of the Year in 2021, Alan Ranger, describes the design stage of the photographic process as a key juncture in the photographer's development.[3] This phase is not about following textbook rules or coloring within the lines, but learning how to account for every detail within a frame and remaining teachable enough to consider why the image is valuable at all. The next phase of Gordon's life would be a demolition site where building the foundation of the man would require pulling down the broken framework within him, with the intent of assembling a new one.

Johnson believes the leaders we admire most are often those who have endured great hardship.[4] Their stories, filled with turbulence and trial, serve as a light in a tunnel of darkness when we cannot see our way out of our own circumstances. Transformational leaders become individuals who role model behavior we strive to function with, but in many instances have yet to possess. What is the gap? How do we close the space between who we desire to become and who we are today? I call this gap the *leader's path*. There is a distance to travel for anyone desiring to become the leader they aspire to become. The images of men and women who shook the nation and, in some cases, the world seem so far away from where we are. So why even bother pursuing something unattainable? My question to you would be, is it truly unattainable? I believe each of us has an innate desire to unlock the next chapter of our growth, and the way to get there is the leader's path.

The Leaders Path

> *Not everyone is willing to trek the path required to become one.*

The leader's path is the journey one must take alone. It is an inward pursuit of an outward expression that requires discipline, commitment, and purpose. For the leader to be willing to take this journey, purpose must be in the tank to sustain the trek. Kouzes & Posner believe the domain of leaders is the future.[5] Translated, they are obsessed with the journey because they believe there is a destination they need to prepare themselves and others for. Discipline and commitment could be considered interchangeable, but for the purposes of defining the leader's path, let's explore them a bit further. A leader who is not committed to fulfilling a purpose is not leading but aimlessly exploring. This manifests itself as high activity for its own sake. Our calendars can be full, and our time can be sparse, but if we're not focusing on what's important, then we may believe we're making progress when in fact we are running in place. I learned that if I'm on a treadmill, I can lose weight, sweat, and even have trouble. What I will not experience is the challenges of the weather or the uneven terrain, coupled with exposure to the outdoors. Thank you, *Peloton*.

Which leads to discipline. Gourani suggests that transformation of any kind is not sporadic or random but is the result of meticulous discipline and structure.[6] The leader's path requires a level of discipline to build the capacity fit for the type of leadership that individual will be in. The level of discipline required to be a frontline manager may not be the same as that required of the CEO, given the levels and types of opposition they both will inherently face. This principle applies to us as well. The leader's path is not for everyone, which is why everyone has the potential to become a leader. But the reality is that not everyone is willing to trek the path required to become one.

Gordon would go on to become close friends with hardship. He would be chiseled through spells of homelessness, extreme poverty, inconsistent employment, and uncertainty in his commitment to his own education. He endured racism, heartache, hunger pains, and the pain of the cold. His anger would be released in moments, such as killing a huge rat in Harlem with his shoes after being bitten.[7] Up until this moment in Gordon's life, there appeared to be nothing resonant of a promising future, but the design of life also accounts for timing. In 1933, President Roosevelt began a program designed for impoverished youth in America called the Civilian Conservation Corps.[7] The program would give individuals like Gordon the opportunity to earn a decent wage of $30 per month while working in areas such as road construction, reforestation, and soil erosion.[1] This was an opportunity that would mark a major transition in the life of Gordon Parks.

The challenging upbringing Gordon endured yielded him a maturity unlike that of his peers in the corps. Gordon had effectively been on his own navigating life since he was fifteen, and at this moment, he was twenty-one and on the verge of starting a family with his new wife.[1] Gordon would go on to take several different jobs after his service in the corps as he continued to look for the means to support his family. While serving on the North Coast Limited train, he was exposed to how the wealthy lived, and while cleaning one of the cars during a run, he came across a portfolio of photographs that would change his life trajectory.[1] These images ignited something deep within him as if they gave voice to the pain within him while simultaneously giving life to his purpose. Gordon would remember the photographers' names and begin studying their work. He was fascinated by what he learned, which led him to explore art and cinema further. Eventually he was exposed to a photographer who risked his life filming a Japanese fighter attacking an American gunboat.[1] The photographer came on stage after the short film to a rousing applause, which pulled on the heartstrings of Gordon. A few days later, he would purchase his first camera from a local pawn shop, which would accelerate events.

New Beginnings

Gordon began practicing photography with no formal training, only a passion in his heart. He somehow found the resolve to pursue a dream regardless of the lot he had been dealt. This led him to approach a fashion store owner and ask to shoot retail clothing. To his surprise, he was given an opportunity that led to another, and another. Eventually, he found himself the recipient of a fellowship awarded to promising black and southern white students.[1] Gordon was breaking barriers without realizing it at the time, as he was the first ever photographer to receive such an award. This fellowship paid him $200 per month and brought him to Washington, DC, to serve with the Farm Security Administration.[1]

The third stage of the photographic process is known as the enhancement stage. This is where photos are edited, and the photographer is given the opportunity to identify what they did see, or what they did not see that needs to be seen.[3] For the transformational leader, the enhancement of individuals' self-efficacy is paramount to their success.[2] An individual's concept of self is influenced by the competent transformational leader whom they identify with as trustworthy.[2] When you and I can see the willingness in a leader to remain a lifelong learner who is open to feedback and agile enough to adjust to new findings, we are witnessing transformational leadership. Their actions and lifestyle serve as an influential model that inspires trust and helps exceed one's individual expectations.

Enhancing teams, groups, or individuals requires a safe environment where taking risks is an acceptable part of the culture. Brown suggests that leaders who are trained in resilience proactively are inherently more courageous and less risk-averse because they view falling or failure as a necessary part of the process rather than a mistake.[8] The confidence to instill this in someone else can only come from a place of authenticity, meaning the leader must experience it before they are in a position to prepare someone else to operate in it. If you are an artist and I have never painted, never studied painting, and never had a conversation with someone in the painting business trying to explain to you how you should be holding the brush when you paint, wouldn't that be considered disingenuous? Unfortunately, this is the reality we live in today. Technology has made everyone an expert in something without establishing credibility. It's as simple as filming a YouTube video about a topic based on a conversation someone had. Transformational leaders not only *talk the talk, but they walk the walk*.

The final stage of the photographic process is to share.[3] The picture has been identified, the overall design has been curated, the photo has been shot, and final edits have been implemented. All that remains is the opportunity to present the finished work to the public. Similarly, the life of a transformational leader on display is what's needed to create exceptional performance today. Change is happening more rapidly today than in the past due to a variety of factors, including cultural shifts, technological acceleration, globalization, and the information age.[9] The workforce demographic has adjusted over the past decade to the point where, by 2050, today's majority groups will become minorities and vice versa. Changes like these require a style of leadership more dynamic and adaptive than traditional models.[9] Kotter believes the fast-moving world we live in requires leaders to engage employees' hearts and minds, and if they are unable to communicate a clear vision and intentions, gaining a competitive edge as an organization will not be attainable.[10]

Next Steps

Transformation is in the way we show up as leaders, the way we listen and communicate as leaders, and the actions we model as leaders. Gordon lived a life filled with obscurity and constant challenges; however, he identified the leader's path, becoming the first African American to hold a full-time staff position as a writer and photographer for America's leading photo magazine, Life. For over twenty years, Gordon would identify the most controversial images and stories to share with the American public, highlighting civil rights, poverty, and war. He was not afraid of conflict, as life had hardened him, preparing him for these moments of exposure. His influence would be lasting as he was named the godfather of Malcolm X's daughter.[1] The community respected his efforts and his story so much that even director Spike Lee is on record that Gordon inspired his efforts after witnessing another black director create films, art and music against unbearable odds.

What can we learn from the life of Gordon Parks as a transformational leader today? We are all aware of traditional ways of leadership, but Gordon reveals to us that leadership can and must become adaptive. In many cases, change is approached as a singular event, when in reality it is perpetual. Life sometimes paints with broad strokes, but each situation carries its own nuance, and every leader and follower bears a story that gives context into who they are. If we view everyone at face value, we rob ourselves of the treasure of building genuine relationships and learning from one another's history. Lastly, we can either manage people or build them. Mayberry suggests that historically, controlling management was not only the right way to lead but was also considered crucial to many leaders' effectiveness.[11] This dynamic no longer exists today. It is a damaging practice that has repercussions far outweighing the return on your investment in time and development.[11] Transformational leaders discern that excellence is fostered in an environment conducive to building rather than tearing down.

Elevation in Practice

Practical elevation requires:

- *Delegation* - trusting others with authority and responsibility.

- *Empowerment* - equipping people with skills, resources, and confidence.

- *Sustainability* - building structures and cultures that reinforce leadership principles.

Elevation requires patience and vision. It often means stepping back so others can step forward.

Rise In Action

- Delegation Audit - write down three responsibilities you currently hold. Which one could you entrust to someone else this month?

- Empowerment Exercise - Identify one person you will resource, coach, or sponsor to take the next step in their growth.

- Legacy Reflection - Ask yourself, *what will remain when I am gone?*

Elevation is the pinnacle of the R.I.S.E. framework. When leaders elevate, then ensure that their influence multiplies, their culture endures, and their legacy continues. Leadership is not about how brightly you shine; it's about how many others shine because of you. To reflect, inspire, serve, and elevate is to live as a transformational leader whose rise empowers others.

1. Parks, G. (1966). A Choice of Weapons. Harper & Row.

2. Allender, D.B. (2006). Leading With a Limp. Waterbrook Press.

3. Ranger, A. (2023). 5 Stages To Improve Your Photography / A Professional Guide. https://www.alanranger.com/

4. Johnson, C.E. (2018). Meeting the Ethical Challenges of Leadership: Casting Light or Shadow 7th edition. SAGE Publications, Inc.

5. Kouzes, J.M., & Posner, B.Z. (2017). The Leadership Challenge 6th edition. John Wiley & Sons, Inc.

6. Gourani, S. (2024). Why Discipline Outshines Motivation For Effective Leadership. Forbes Magazine.

7. Parks, G. (1912). Voices in the Mirror an Autobiography. Bantam Doubleday Dell Publishing Group, Inc.

8. Brown, B. (2018). Dare to Lead. Random House.

9. Sosik, J.J., & Jung, D. (2018). Full Range Leadership Development. Routledge.

10. Kotter, J.P. (1996). Leading Change. Harvard Business Review Press.

11. Mayberry, M. (2024). The Transformational Leader: How the world's best leaders build teams, inspire action, and achieve lasting success. John Wiley & Sons, Inc.

PART II - Rising in Contexts

Chapter 6

R.I.S.E. in the Classroom: Leadership in the Classroom

> "You cannot escape the responsibility of tomorrow by evading it today."
>
> Abraham Lincoln

EDUCATION IS NOT SIMPLY about teaching information; it's shaping identity. Every student carries untapped potential, and every classroom has the power to cultivate leaders who will one day influence nations, industries, and communities. When we apply the R.I.S.E. framework in schools, we shift education from compliance to transformation, from teaching *what* to think to guiding *how* to lead.

The words of the former President of the United States from 1864, during a tumultuous time in America, were not only a great quote but also a prophetic declaration that has rippled through the ages. The Civil War was a moment in our history that, if we could press the rewind button, I am sure we would start over. The ground in America is filled with the blood of young men fighting each other over ideas. These ideas of independence from the union, reunification, and the abolition of slavery were so dangerous, so against the grain, and so radical that they caused a nation to divide itself overnight. Lincoln assumed the presidency in March 1861, facing a seemingly impossible task: leading a nation in the midst of chaos back to stability.[1] As he reflected, he knew he needed key individuals around him to navigate this moment, so he selected a cabinet composed of men with greater intelligence, wealth, and social status than his own.[1] An outsider looking in could have easily assumed his decision would end with him forfeiting his presidency, but his choice did just the opposite. Lincoln leveraged some of the best minds and leaders of the day to his advantage, using them as data points to inform his service to the nation. Lincoln faced difficult decisions that would affect many. Despite this challenge, he was able to inspire his cabinet to identify with something much larger than themselves.[1] He called for sacrifice from himself and others as they pursued higher goals that saw beyond that moment in time. Lincoln elevated that group of men, showing after many failures that he had been uniquely built for that moment in time to lead our nation.

It has always been interesting to see how someone's life pursuits prepare them for an unexpected moment, as if there was a pre-written destiny or assignment set aside only for them to fulfill. Every day, teachers, professors, mentors, and caretakers are charged with preparing the next generation of world leaders. Educators have a choice to see beyond a child's challenges today and embrace their potential for tomorrow. This assignment is one I've seen many approach with sobriety and others with frustration. In either case, the seeds we plant today in our school systems, we will reap tomorrow.

The Greek philosopher Epictetus once said, "Circumstances don't make the man, they only reveal him to himself." This statement could not be truer when you consider the life of Eunice Hunton Carter. If you are anything like me, this may be the first time you are hearing this woman's name. Growing up, being able to explore the lives of prominent minority figures in school remained limited to the likes of Martin Luther King and Malcolm X. Beyond these men, I was ill-informed of the historical impact other minority figures had throughout time, including Eunice. She was not only the first black woman to simultaneously earn her bachelor's and master's degrees at Smith University, but she would go on to become the first black woman to serve in the New York Prosecutor's Office.[2]

Right now, you may be thinking that's an interesting fact, but I still don't see the full connection between her life and the transformational principles for the classroom. That's fair, and I thought the same until I had the opportunity to dig a bit deeper into her life.

What I found was a woman who was a double minority, navigating both the challenges of being a woman and being black in an environment predominantly filled with white males, and the resistance she had to face. While her story in no way ended here, one of the chief highlights of her life was her boldness to stand against the mob and, more specifically, Lucky Luciano. It would be her willingness to research, review, and think critically that would eventually lead to a break in one of the greatest cases known in law. But before we connect the dots, we need to take a step back.

Born to Fly

As Carter introduces us to Eunice, she is a child growing up in Atlanta, blocks away from a White Mob angry with black business owners advancing economically and other black individuals seemingly taking jobs and making wages traditionally set aside for whites.[3] Eunice's parents were affluent and considered by many to be two of the most influential black activists in Atlanta.[3] However, the risk was too much for them to bear, which led them to migrate up north with hopes of making a larger impact and increasing the overall safety of their family. Eunice's mother, Addie, was a prominent activist with a clear message, educating groups on the barriers impacting not only race but also gender.[2] She was bold, courageous, and fearless in her delivery. All characteristics that would prove to be necessary for the challenges ahead for her daughter.

William Hunton, Eunice's father, was well known for his impact with establishing the YMCA nationally. His work as a secretary often left him on the road, traveling frequently not being as present with his family as he would have liked.[3] However, his work ethic, gained from his father, a former slave turned skilled blacksmith, became a critical piece of his DNA. William grew up as a boy with great discipline, chores, cleaning and running errands became part of his weekly routine.[3] These actions built in him a sense of process, giving him a systematic approach to everything he encountered. That same level of detail and logic-oriented thinking would come in handy for his daughter Eunice throughout her career.

Kouzes & Posner suggest success in business and in life ultimately depends on how well we know ourselves, our values, and our why.[4] Why do we value what we value? This is a key question to uncovering our need to transform and leaning into our ability to function transformationally. Transformational leadership, at its core, is mission-driven; the absence of a clear objective, aspirational or not, leads to a lack of clarity and a dissipation of movement. The leader's responsibility is to create an environment where others can recognize the value of what needs to be accomplished and, specifically, how their actions impact the outcome. Simplifying what is complex for many into what is simple for all.

The legal profession is matrixed, filled with varying opinions, perspectives, tactics, and experiences, which can bias how certain subjects are approached. Eunice was built to navigate the treacherous terrain ahead of her time, given the level of exposure from her past. Often, we find ourselves, as leaders, in scenarios where we're challenged to fit into someone else's ideology of what good looks like, instead of embracing our uniqueness. The transformational leader I'm referring to is one with a high sense of self-awareness. They are aware enough to leverage all their story, including the good, bad, and the ugly, with the intent of impacting others to become or accomplish more than they believed could be done. This leader is not a conformist but an individualist. This is why it leads them to function counter-culturally to some but purposeful to them. Modeling this behavior in schools and campuses provides students with the space to explore. When leadership returns to a posture where the goal isn't to be liked to influence but to provide influence because it's the right thing to do, we will see transformation.

Curiosity

Eunice's journey was purposeful, but an outsider looking in could easily have misinterpreted her career decisions as haphazard. The adage that career progression is not always linear was the story of Eunice. A master's degree recipient turned teacher, turned social worker, turned political candidate displayed a sincere work ethic and willingness to learn new things.[3] Thomas Dewey, New York state appointed special prosecutor and former interim US Attorney, recognized the talented perspective someone like Eunice could offer in support of his quest to clean up New York.[3] As Thomas assembled his team, he, being a white male, influenced himself to the forming of a homogeneous team of like minds and perspectives, and later realized the challenge ahead of him would require diversity of thought. Eunice was positioned solely as an individual on the team with keen insight into the crime in New York City. Her connection to the area, the people, and the culture would give them a competitive advantage as they approached the insurmountable task of taking down the mob.

Up to that point, the state had had minimal success prosecuting prominent mob figures, as they bribed many political figures, judges, and law enforcement officials at various levels to protect them as they continued their business affairs.[3] In all honesty, Thomas, as motivated as he was to assemble this dream team of lawyers, he too was unsure of the ultimate outcome. But throughout the transition, amid the media noise and overwhelming confusion, Eunice remained steadfast. So much so that she remembered her days prosecuting prostitutes in NYC's magistrates court and recalled that many of those brought into her office were represented by the same attorney and the same bail bondsmen.[3] She suspected then that there may be some way to link the mob with prostitution throughout the city, but she would need time to gather the requisite evidence to support her hypothesis.[3] This mindset was completely contrary to Thomas and the team of lawyers, but Eunice had been accustomed to living life against the grain, giving her tough skin to swim against the current.

Eunice would spend hours dedicated to reviewing documents and different records of prostitution in hopes of gathering data necessary to draw a connection.[3] As her discovery went further, she uncovered the name of the lawyer who represented the majority of the prostitutes in court and noticed the applications for bail were always signed by the same group of individuals.[3] Her confidence grew as she was beginning to identify something bigger than she could have anticipated. Organized crime in the 30's was a clear problem that law enforcement could not solve. Individuals like Dutch Schultz, known for racketeering and ingratiating himself so deeply into the community, had outmaneuvered law enforcement for years.[3] Thomas was driven to prosecute him so much so that he almost sent him to prison twice, but Dutch was acquitted.[3] Against better judgement and a warning from the FBI, Thomas continued his efforts against Dutch, which drove him to orchestrate an assassination attempt against him.[3] The negative attention the Dutch were creating was becoming a distraction to business, which led to the introduction of Lucky Luciano into the picture, who used a strategy for personal gain. Lucky saw Dutch's actions as a threat that would cause greater harm than benefit, so he ensured the Dutch would no longer live to cause any further interruptions.[3] While the closure of Dutch was a relief to Thomas, it only adjusted their focus to Lucky moving forward. As fate would have it, the key to cracking the code on organized crime in New York was slowly coming together during the power transition in the underground world.[3]

When Lucky was found guilty, Eunice's celebrity skyrocketed. She received an honorary doctoral degree in law from Northampton College in Massachusetts, a prestigious honor for a black woman.[3] Eunice would continue to serve in the public sector, with Thomas elevating his brand while simultaneously elevating her own image in the public eye.

New Beginnings

> *A transformational leader sees potential in pain.*

Eventually, Eunice decided it was time to leave the public sector and began her own private practice as a partnership that provided counsel through a public relations firm focused on supporting minorities.[3] With the freedom to pursue her own passions, Eunice became an elder stateswoman fighting for social justice and often choosing to support initiatives that her supporters were not aligned with.[3] Her determination, career work ethic, exposure for minority women, and continued fight for equality spiked the number of women interested in law, causing more women to obtain their law degrees and jump into the field. This did not come from her explicitly telling women there is a need for more representation in this area, but rather from her entire life serving as a clear picture of the possibility of becoming something more, doing something more, and influencing something more.

I once heard a man make a statement that resonated with me so deeply, I never forgot it. The speaker said we are the sum total of our decisions. Take a moment to let that to sink in. Chew on it, then digest it. When I first heard this comment, I immediately thought to myself that my excuses no longer matter. Sure, I could easily make the case that I was where I was in life because of my childhood upbringing. I had a mother who wrestled with bipolarism all my existence with her. The weight of depression some days was resonant to a bookbag filled with bricks. My father was physically present but emotionally absent. My older siblings were already out of the house, so I was left to internalize my anger and my frustration. My decisions were influenced by my low self-worth, leading me to seek approval from my peers.

This is the story of your typical youth in America today. Our ability to communicate with one another has been hampered by technology leaving us with accountability and character deficits in leadership at all levels and facets of life. Why do I share this story, you might ask? I want you to see that, regardless of the challenges we face, we are responsible for the decisions we make. Transformational leaders own their decisions even when they have minimal buy-in from others. What gives them the ability to stand on principle regardless of the backlash they receive? The common thread throughout time and even now in those we see exemplify the steadfastness we admire is their ability to see beyond today. Inspiration in the hands of an educator is a more powerful tool than a pencil. Why, you may ask? In those formative years of growth, what we remember most is how people made us feel, not the information they gave us. That teacher's aide who noticed the student sitting by themselves during lunch and showed kindness by offering their time to let that student feel seen will not be easily forgotten. Barna believes vision is something that stretches our abilities by dreaming the most possible dream, undergirded by great depth and understanding of potential, knowledge, and facts.[5] A transformational leader sees potential in pain.

The transformational leader functions in a dynamic world filled with volatility, which requires flexibility. That is what makes these types of leaders so inspiring. They share a hunger for continuous improvement and a drive for change which reveals itself through their relentless pursuit of growth. I have come across individuals who challenge the notion that anyone can become a transformational leader. I enjoy these moments of enlightenment about our broken state. To simplify the transformational element, I simply ask How did you get here? Consider that we were once a combination of sperm and an egg that underwent a transformation that, nine months later, produced a child. That same child went through several transformations from youth to adolescence to young adulthood to adulthood. Each stage bears with it a separate set of responsibilities as we grow into different levels of maturity.

Transformation is alive and well, and sometimes has been hidden by our choices or beliefs. We have all witnessed, or will witness, someone in our lifetime whose influence transcends the moment. As if they were handcrafted for it. Some of us will be that individual faced with an opportunity to function in fight, flight, or freeze. I remember managing a team of roughly 500 individuals at Madison Square Garden (MSG), preparing for another sold-out concert where we would serve approximately 20,000 people with food, drinks, and merchandise over a 4-hour period. My director decided to take the evening off and communicated to senior leadership that if there is an emergency, they should contact me. I didn't think anything of it, as emergencies that require that type of contact are rare during an event. But this night was different. Fifteen minutes into the show, the power went out in the building and the surrounding area, ten city blocks each way. There was alcohol, cash, and people unaccounted for, and an emergency evacuation was being ordered by our security team. My colleagues approached me with panic and disbelief, questioning how we would handle the situation. It was in that moment as if everything around me slowed down. I had clarity, I had peace, and I had a plan. Can I explain why there was a sobriety upon me in that moment that my colleagues did not have? No. What I can tell you is that within a few minutes, we had a clear plan of action, objectives, and we had ensured everything was accounted for in what we were about to execute.

As I dispersed the other leaders on the floor with the next steps, I received a phone call. It was the SVP & GM of Operations, not looking to see how we were doing or the temperament of one of the largest teams in building. He wanted to know that we had a plan, and there was a sense of urgency in his tone as I explained what we had already set in motion. Once he heard our plan, he became more responsive and more human. I didn't know at the time, but he had called several other department heads before me, and they were scrambling to put something together without establishing clear roles and responsibilities for carrying out a full building dismissal. I learned something in that moment. I learned that my willingness to listen, remain coachable, and inspire others to exceed their own expectations was fully activated in this instance, and that what we collectively accomplished was beyond what any of us could have accomplished on our own. We ended up getting everyone out of the building safely, accounting for every cash drawer, all mobile cash units from our vendors, all waste, and all alcohol with pencils and paper. We simplified our closing procedures and identified what needed to be prioritized that evening and what could be done later.

Transformational moments are not always as clear to us when they are in process, but reflection yields lessons we can apply in the future. Always remaining in a posture of learning and readiness, with the intent to improve, is what transformational leaders express. Eunice was a woman who embodied these characteristics her entire life, and her preparation, too, was a catalyst for her when her moment arrived. Vision casting is not something leaders do in vain, but it is provides a north star for a circumstance you haven't arrived at yet. If the leader's focus remains on continuous improvement, when the moment arrives, it will not be a surprise to you but a privilege you get to partake in.

*Eunice Hunton Carter - A **R.I.S.E.** Model for Education*

Eunice Hunton Carter's story serves as a bridge between empowerment and education. Born into an era of limited opportunity, she reflected on her purpose, inspired others through brilliance and perseverance, served through justice, and elevated future generations. Her life reminds us, as students and educators, that leadership begins with self-awareness and culminates in service.

Reflect: Building Self-Awareness in Students

Before students can lead, they must understand themselves. Reflection cultivates curiosity, emotional intelligence, and a sense of ownership over learning.

Practical Examples:

- Journal - "What does success mean to me?" or "What do I stand for?"

- Classroom check-ins where students set weekly goals and reflect on progress.

- Educators model vulnerability by sharing their own reflections.

When students learn to reflect, they stop comparing themselves to others and begin to discover the leader within.

Inspire: Cultivating Vision and Belief

Inspiration bridges self-discovery and action. Teachers who model belief ignite belief. It is not only what we teach, but how we teach. Our energy, empathy, and vision all work together to shape students' futures.

Practical Examples:

- Teachers share personal stories of perseverance.

- Class projects are built around "What problem can you

solve in your school?"

- Guest speakers who embody possibility

Students rarely remember the content of a lecture, but they always remember how a teacher made them feel.

Serve: Empowering Students to Lead Through Service

Service transforms classrooms into communities. When students serve, they learn humility, empathy, and the value of contribution over competition.

Practical Examples:

- Peer mentoring programs
- Service-learning projects tied to curriculum goals
- Team-based activities that reward collaboration, not just achievement

The greatest lesson a student can learn is that leadership is not about being first; it's about bringing others with you.

Elevate: Sustaining a Culture of Leadership

Elevation happens when leadership becomes part of the school's DNA. When educators and administrators design systems that encourage student ownership, leadership continues even when individuals move on.

Practical Examples:

- Student-led assemblies or advisory groups
- Leadership electives focused on R.I.S.E. principles.

- Recognition systems that celebrate mentorship and growth

The measure of great education is not the grades left behind, but the leaders carried forward.

Self-Reflection: Walking the Walk

- How do I currently model reflection and self-awareness in my classroom?
- When was the last time I shared my personal "why" with my students?
- What opportunities exist in my school for students to lead, serve, and elevate others?

When schools adopt the R.I.S.E. framework, they no longer just educate; they transform. Every lesson becomes a leadership opportunity, and every student becomes a catalyst for change. The next generation is not waiting to be told they can lead; they're waiting to be shown how.

---

1. Goodwin, D.K. (2018). Leadership in Turbulent Times. Simon & Schuster.

2. Li, Y. & Greenwald, M.S. (2021). A Lifelong Fight for Social Justice. Fordham University Press.

3. Carter, S.L. (2018). Invisible. Macmillan Publishing Group.

4. Kouzes, J.M., & Posner, B.Z. (2010). The Truth About Leadership. John Wiley & Sons, Inc.

5. Barna, G. (2018). The Power of Vision 3rd edition. Baker Books.

CHAPTER 7

R.I.S.E. in Business: Leadership Beyond Profit

"Life is either a daring adventure or nothing at all."
Helen Keller

LEADERSHIP IN BUSINESS HAS long been measured by numbers, quarterly returns, margins, and market share. Yet, in today's world, the organizations that rise above the rest are not those driven solely by profit, but by purpose. When leaders embrace R.I.S.E., they create workplaces where people are not managed but motivated, where strategy is human-centered, and where growth becomes both measurable and meaningful. The R.I.S.E. framework transforms the way organizations operate by aligning values, vision, service, and sustainability, the four cornerstones of modern leadership.

Architecture is a detailed process related to the design, planning, and sketching of a structure. If you are looking to make significant home improvements, consulting someone with this skillset would be wise. As part of that process, the architect would review the drawings or the structure's blueprint. The blueprint tells the story others cannot see. It's the visual representation of the original intent of the structure under observation. I remember opening a new restaurant and reviewing the blueprints to confirm that all items were being placed according to the plan. The open kitchen required a certain distance between the grill and the sink to ensure enough space for movement during peak service periods. After many months of labor and preparation, we were ready to open and had a line around the corner in Bay Ridge, Brooklyn.

Although this experience will never be forgotten, I am fully aware that this opportunity came about because a previous restaurant in the same location closed. Essentially, if it had not been for the previous property owner laying a solid foundation for us to build on, the process would have been significantly more difficult. We took what was and reconstructed it into what could be. Many of us are in the situations we are in because of those who have gone before us in our family, in society, in all facets of life. When we consider the life of Max Robinson, we cannot tell his transformational story without acknowledging how he paved the way for others to follow. The Oxford Dictionary defines reconstruction as the rebuilding of something after it has been damaged or destroyed. That definition encapsulates Max's life. It also epitomizes business agility. James Canton, the CEO of the Institute for Global Futures, believes innovation has become the chief competitive advantage for businesses, and those who embrace it will thrive while those who resist will perish.[1]

Max was born in Richmond, Virginia, in 1939 with the desire to become a television news anchor. Of all the potential career paths Max could choose, this one was telling of his bold personality and willingness to stand up to opposition. In 1959, after attending Oberlin College, Virginia Union University, and Indiana University, he received his first opportunity to be on television, only to be told he must read the news while hidden from the public on camera.[2] Can you imagine what it would feel like if your entire life you had to deal with prejudice, self-doubt, and animosity from others, feeling as though you had to prove your value at every turn, only to get the opportunity you've been waiting for and to have it stripped from you in the same moment?

Max, disappointed but not broken, had one of several choices to make. Fight, flight, or freeze. Max chose to fight for what he believed in and removed the slide covering him from the camera so that his voice could be heard and his face could be seen. This resulted in his immediate firing the next day. The experience would prove telling for Max as his values pushed him to act when others remained silent. That same posture would be embedded in Max's life story and reveal itself in other facets of his life.

Transformed For Purpose

Transformation is a process. It is the transition from one state to something else completely different. The essence of transformational leadership is internal evolution rather than external validation.[3] Mayberry suggests this type of leadership transcends industries and locations.[2] It represents a leadership that will not be limited by circumstance but reveals itself through resiliency. Transformational leaders are not meant to fit into traditional models or modes. They are meant to produce change and activate dormant potential in others. While these types of individuals are typically purpose-driven, their lives model selflessness.

Max lived a life filled with paradox. In one area of his life, his pursuit in media as a black man paved the way for many. His influence impacted many who witnessed him overcome opposition and remain steadfast. However, Max lived a shorter life than he would have anticipated. At forty-nine years of age, Max had openly wrestled against prejudice, alcohol abuse, career disaster, and three failed marriages.[4] But in his silence, there was suffering. In his silence, there was unspoken pain and frustration. In his silence, there was an unhealed trauma that would only come to the surface after his death.

Upon Max's death, it was discovered that in addition to the adversity he dealt with, he also had AIDS. The revelation of this finding left many closest to him perplexed. The public was discouraged due to not hearing him acknowledge openly that he had contracted AIDS. The sentiment during that moment was based on data that overwhelmingly cited those who contracted the disease were primarily homosexual or bisexual men.[3] Both of which Max would never claim as true while he lived. Instead, Max had a burning passion to advocate for racial justice in America and wanted his legacy to reflect that. Cuniberti reflects that one of Max's most triumphant moments occurred when he was a child, showing his unwillingness to give in to prejudice by drinking from a white-only water fountain.[3]

Let's Paint the Picture

For context, Max began his journey on television in 1959 during the height of the Jim Crow era. For a black man to be on television during this moment in time was not only unheard of but essentially impossible. Max, however, was a trailblazer. He not only challenged the status quo through his television appearances, but his actions on and off camera also showed the intentions of his heart. Max had no fear of challenging executives at large networks to ensure a balanced perspective on how the African American community was depicted on camera.

Kouzes & Posner believe that challenge is the crucible for greatness.[5] When you examine this statement further and consider your own life, you can probably remember certain situations that called for a higher version of yourself to overcome an obstacle. I have experienced this dynamic at every stage of my life, from adolescence to adulthood. But I remember one situation that will stay with me for the rest of my life. I was 32 years old when I married my wife, Stephanie. She and I had been through a number of challenges together, and little did we know we were only scratching the surface of the crucible that produces greatness.

On the night of our rehearsal dinner before we got married, there was a moment that brought a level of sobriety to my heart and mind, and I will share it with my sons when they are prepared to make a similar type of commitment. That evening, as we stood at the altar, walking through the ceremony's nuances, I felt a weight fall on my shoulders. It wasn't a heaviness, but it felt as if I was being given a jacket tailor-made for me to walk in that I couldn't see but sensed strongly. Later that evening, in my private time, I asked God what that was, and a thought bubbled up in my heart. The thought was that I was being entrusted with someone special, and that it would require an approach, a sensitivity, a level of focus that I had yet to function in with any consistency.

As I woke up the next morning, my jitters were gone, all apprehension or doubt had left, and I stood at the altar waiting for my bride with a confidence knowing that I was not alone but entrusted to serve at a higher level. Upon returning to our apartment from our honeymoon, Stephanie began to cry and it was in that moment that I understood what had happened to me at the altar. She was realizing that she would no longer be returning to her mother and father, but that we had been charged to begin a committed life together. As I embraced her, she discerned the responsibility in my eyes, and her anxiety began to dissipate. I share this story to highlight that, as leaders, sometimes we will not know when our moment will arrive, but we will all come face-to-face with our values and commitments, which will require us to make a decision. The transformational leader embraces these moments and anticipates them, preparing for something new.

The Challenge of Transformation

As with any transformation, the expectation should never be immediate. A baby is conceived and takes, on average, 9 months to develop. Yeast takes roughly 1.5 to 2 hours to fully rise, and there is a popular HGTV show where they commit to building a house from the ground up in 100 days. The common thread in all these examples is the process of time. The process of change is a paradox that all leaders will eventually face according to McIntosh & Rima.[6] In the life of a leader, there are experiences that uniquely shape who they are. McIntosh & Rima reference the relational friction, external challenges, and personal pain placed on the leader, leaving them with the option of identifying a solution through their internal search or remaining in a stagnant state because they were unwilling to uproot old mindsets and paradigms to embrace something new.[5]

A hindrance to our ability to transform is our inability to identify the moment it exists in. Transformational people and opportunities are not always present, or they are misinterpreted, leaving us blind to their impact. Consider how many individuals were not in agreement with a former businessman who did things differently from their predecessors. Take Jack Welch, the late CEO of GE. Jack took over the company when it was in serious financial trouble, only to emerge on the other side, defying the odds so significantly that he is known by many as the CEO of the century. Jack's tactical leadership was so different that it pushed those around him to stretch themselves beyond their own capabilities, only to recognize they were, in fact, able.

Jack instituted a company-wide mandate requiring all organizations within his purview to either become the number one or number two based business in the industry, or he would get rid of them. To many, this may seem harsh, but to those within his company, it proved to be the launching pad for a billion-dollar brand, as Jack saw profits triple in a short period, giving him access to levels of influence with the board and the organization he wasn't accustomed to.

When we view individuals, whether on our teams, in the restaurants, or in the boardroom, as just common, we forfeit the moment to connect with someone who today may not carry the influence we would like them to have, only to find out one day they will have the influence we will need. Jack's leadership priorities and vision were so clear and direct that they produced several Fortune 500 CEOs in the coming years. Influence for transformational leaders is not a luxury but a priority for survival. Mayberry suggests that transformational leadership is not based solely on expertise but also on our ability to inspire.[2]

What is Your Story

Have you ever listened to a story that was so captivating and engaging that it kept you interested the entire time? I'm hopeful you're experiencing one now. What were the elements of that story that resonated with you most? Was it the setting, the speaker's tone, the content, or the timing? Each of these categories, and plenty more, could be the catalyst for a story that has that kind of impact on us. When I hear stories in a way that lets me hear what's not being said, I am pulled in. It's not necessarily due to the way the story is being told, but rather to the authenticity the story holds for the speaker. Truth is a rare commodity in society today, which makes it that much more valuable when it's present.

In a recent conversation with a peer about workplace resilience, I was introduced to the reality that each of us carries a significant story that makes us unique and gives us value internally. Our individual stories, however tragic, challenging, or blessed, have molded us with a certain countenance while enabling us to do what is distinctive to us. The key action step here is to embrace it. The caterpillar with dreams of becoming a butterfly one day embraces the process of change despite the danger. The eaglet thrown out of the nest by its parents, only to be caught right before it hits the ground, must embrace the process of change. What makes human beings any different? Transformation is an equal opportunist. It carries no bias and thrives in diverse situations.

Equal Opportunity

> *What if our scars as leaders were not seen as disqualifiers but mobilizers?*

When we leverage our personal stories as the foundation that built us rather than the structure that prevents us from reaching our potential, we gain access to the power of true transformation. *The ability to transform others.* When you have been transformed, you gain insight into an experience that those you encounter have yet to participate in. Your interactions become more authentic when grounded in truth rather than theory alone. Consider the redwood trees of California. These are among the largest trees in the world, growing upwards of 300 feet tall. Beautiful to see and a wonder to experience, but what is even more intriguing to me is what does not get much attention. The root system underground reaches deep. The other trees within the forest hold each other together underground, so when storms come, those trees don't even budge. Because of the depth of their roots, they are able to flourish and help others do the same.

The same principle applies to the transformational leader. The depth of the individual's transformational experience equips them to empower others to reach their full potential. Bass & Riggio suggest these leaders build trust through the consistency and equity they model with those they influence.[7] To the transformational leader, every individual they encounter is observed as an opportunity to serve. The follower's social class, demographic, sex, or age holds no bearing on the transformational leader because the goal always remains the same. Change in the young person struggling to find their identity will look different than the CEO of a Fortune 500 company, but the impact of internal transformation would be the same.

Everyone is concerned with the outward appearance of transformational leadership, but is less focused on its roots. What if our scars as leaders were not seen as disqualifiers but mobilizers? What if our pain wasn't seen as a limitation but a reference? What if publicly our story wasn't seen as an embarrassment but as a clarity-giving entity? If we, as leaders, were able to recognize these moments with the urgency they deserve, our ability to make a significant impact in the lives of others would increase. I once heard a man say opportunities have an expiration date. What does that mean for the transformational leader? It means we only have a small window to alter someone's destiny with the influence we have been blessed with.

Access to transformational leadership requires transparency. Only when our values are on display for everyone to see will we gain the opportunity to influence others. In the world we live in today, social media provides individuals with platforms to expand their reach. The risk for a transformational leader is standing against the possibility of someone misinterpreting their stance or blatantly disagreeing with it in a way that entitles another audience to critique them. Transformational leadership is not for those trying to win a popularity contest. But if you are willing to defy the odds, break barriers, and initiate true change, then this is a space where we can learn from the past and become one of those leaders who make a lasting impact today. Max was one of those leaders willing to swim upstream during a time of great misunderstanding. His actions paved the way for generations of journalists and inspired authenticity in their reporting.

Business As a Platform For Human Transformation

When leaders lead through R.I.S.E., business outcomes become more than a profession; they become a platform for purpose. Profit is no longer the end goal but the byproduct of alignment, authenticity, and shared growth. Organizations that R.I.S.E. reflect deeply, inspire broadly, serve selflessly, and elevate collectively. They don't just create products, they create progress.

Reflect: Self-Awareness as the Foundation of Strategic Leadership

Before any company can rise, its leaders must first reflect. Reflection in business is not just introspection; it's insight in motion. It means knowing who you are as a leader, why you lead, and how those decisions affect those around you. Reflection is how values become visible, and culture becomes conscious.

Practical Applications:

- Leaders participate in regular 360-degree feedback sessions to identify blind spots.

- Organizations host *pause and plan* days with reflection workshops, during which teams assess alignment between their mission and actions.

- Executives revisit core values quarterly to ensure integrity between words and behavior.

A reflective organization doesn't just grow; it evolves with purpose.

R.I.S.E. Reflection

- What does our success cost, and are we willing to pay that price if it means sacrificing our people or our purpose?

Inspire: Communicating Vision and Building Belief

Inspiration is the currency of influence. When leaders inspire, they transform compliance into commitment. Employees don't rally behind numbers; they rally behind narratives. An inspiring vision turns strategy into movement and employees into advocates.

Practical Applications:

- Leaders share personal stories of resilience and lessons learned from failure.

- Vision statements are revisited collaboratively, ensuring employees see themselves in the story.

- Internal communications (newsletters, townhalls, digital platforms) focus on mission-driven storytelling.

The most powerful leaders are not those who talk the loudest; they're the ones who remind others why their work matters.

R.I.S.E. Reflection

- If your company's story were told today, would people feel inspired to be part of the next chapter?

Serve: Empowering People as the Engine of Progress

Service is the secret strength of sustainable organizations. When leaders serve, they don't diminish authority; they multiply impact. A service-centered leader invests in their people, listens deeply, and fosters an environment where creativity can flourish.

Practical Applications:

- Managers shift from performance reviewers to performance coaches.

- Service-based recognition programs celebrate collaboration, empathy, and mentorship.

- Organizations provide time or funding for employees to serve in their communities.

Service-centered leadership is not soft leadership; it's smart leadership. It builds the kind of trust that drives performance and innovation.

R.I.S.E. Reflection

- Who on my team needs support, not supervision, and how can I provide it this week?

Elevate: Building Systems and Legacies That Last

Elevation in business means designing organizations that outlive individual leaders. It's about succession, sustainability, and scale. When a company elevates, it creates frameworks that ensure leadership is shared, not siloed. Elevation is how vision becomes legacy.

Practical Applications:

- Implement mentorship ladders that intentionally develop successors.

- Design "innovation circles" where cross-functional teams generate solutions beyond departmental lines

- Embed R.I.S.E.-based based leadership competencies into performance reviews and promotion criteria.

True leaders don't build followers; they build other leaders.

---

1. Canton, J. (2015). Future Smart: Managing the Game-Changing Trends That Will Transform Your World. Da Capo Press.

2. White Rose Community TV. (2015, Feb 12). Black History Month Moment - Ron Martin presents Max Robinson: [Video] Max Robinson

3. Mayberry, M. (2024). The Transformational Leader: How the world's best leaders build teams, inspire action, and achieve lasting success. John Wiley & Sons, Inc.

4. Cuniberti, B. (1988). Max Robinson's Silent Struggle With Aids. Los Angeles Times.

5. Kouzes, J.M., & Posner, B.Z. (2010). The Truth About Leadership. John Wiley & Sons, Inc.

6. McIntosh, G.L., & Rima, S.D. (2008). Overcoming the Dark Side of Leadership. Baker Books.

7. Bass, B.M., & Riggio, R.E. (2014). Transformational Leadership 2nd edition. Routledge.

CHAPTER 8

R.I.S.E. in Life and Community: Everyday Leadership

> "Feel the fear and do it anyway"
> Susan Jeffers, PHD.

LEADERSHIP BEGINS WHERE YOU ARE. Leadership doesn't start with a title; it begins with a decision. It's the parent who models patience in chaos, the neighbour who volunteers quietly, the young adult who chooses integrity when no one is watching. In every season and setting, the opportunity to lead is present. Through the R.I.S.E. framework - Reflect, Inspire, Serve, Elevate - leadership becomes not a profession, but a practice. It becomes a way of living that ripples through homes, communities, and generations. Everyday leadership is the invisible thread that holds a community together.

In the jungle, a variety of animals fight daily for survival. Of all these animals, both small and large, there remains one who we consider the king of the jungle. The lion is a special creature that we study, we admire, and we revere, but why? Why is the Lion referred to as King when it is not the most cunning, the strongest, or the fastest animal? What differentiates the lion from everyone else? The famous Disney movie The Lion King gives us a picture of the dominance this apex predator carries.

During the movie, the young lion Simba finds himself in a challenging position away from the pack and in danger with several hyenas. The older hyenas mock him as he attempts to roar to show his courage, as he wants to function like his father. His roar is far from intimidating and even comical to the hyenas, so they ask him to roar again. As he opens his mouth, a deafening sound comes across the airways that freezes the hyenas. This sound came from his father, the king, Mufasa. Fear and panic immediately grip the hyenas as Mufasa asserts his dominance as King. There is a knowing, an inner confidence that, regardless of whether Mufasa is in his territory or not, he believes in his ability and what he is capable of as a lion.

After this situation, in which Mufasa saves his son's life, he pulls him aside and teaches him a lesson about authority. As Simba grows into a lion, he faces a choice. Do I become what I know I am created to be and accept the risk of failure, or do I settle for a life of comfort and ease? Simba's decision is undergirded by the need to overcome his fear of transformation. Deep down on the inside, Simba knew he was called to do more and be more in his life, but he also knew what it would require was costly. It would require him to face his past failures and accept them as learning opportunities. It would require him to embrace a version of himself that he had yet to fully experience. It would require for him to remain agile and adapt to the environment of the unknown, where things would no longer be predictable. It would also require Simba to acknowledge that his life trajectory was limiting his potential and hindering him from becoming who he was created to become.

Fear

I have heard fear once defined as false evidence appearing real. The appearance of something as real often is enough to keep people from fulfilling their potential. Imagine yourself wanting to become an entrepreneur. You have dreamt about it, thought about it, imagined what life could be if you mustered enough courage to give it a shot. You are finally ready to begin writing your business plan, and you tell a friend your business idea. Instead of providing you with encouragement and affirmation for the idea you have, they highlight all the challenges you will face if you were to try, and they discredit your idea.

In your own embarrassment, you regretfully agree that your idea may not be the right one to get started, so you place your dream and your idea on a shelf. This is so disappointing, and I have personally experienced this in the past. I have allowed others to question my ideas by presenting me with foreseen obstacles as the evidence appearing real in those moments. In hindsight, what I didn't realise is that those challenges, although they could very well materialise in the future, hadn't happened up to that point. Essentially, I allowed the opinions of others to detour me from a road I had yet to travel and in many cases, neither had they.

I learned a valuable lesson from those experiences. Fear surrounds and influences all of us, but it is my decision that will stand, not my feelings. I can be experiencing a level of fear and choose to move forward, move backwards, or remain paralysed. Gay Hendricks refers to this as the "Upper Limit Problem".[1] The upper limit problem occurs when an individual reaches a point of exploration, creativity, innovation, or anything good that exceeds their upper limit, which is their threshold of comfort. Once this barrier is broken, the individual engages in self-sabotaging behaviour to return to a place of familiarity in their expression and thinking.[1] WOW!

If we allow our unwarranted fears to dictate our decision-making, we are agreeing to lives of limitation. What if there was a different way? What if we were able to consistently align our actions, thoughts and beliefs with fearlessness? This journey we have been on towards transformation has the potential to carry stowaways. Many times, they go unknown, but they have always been present. When we make a commitment to realise our full potential, our egos get deported. Our ego and our concern with how others perceive us have killed more dreams within people than any other medical epidemic known to mankind. The disease of unfulfilled purpose exists only because of our inaccurate perspective on fear.

Open My Eyes

When you are in a fog, your vision is impaired. In the northeastern US, this perspective often occurs. Commuters are on their way to work early in the morning, parents are dropping off their children at school, and others are attending to responsibilities, and in every instance, their activities are hindered by a lack of visual clarity. Notice, in each of these examples, there is movement. When we cannot see clearly, our acceleration becomes bound. As a leader looking to explore and become a transformational leader, vision becomes paramount.

Nick Saban, the former head coach of the Alabama Crimson Tide and the most-winningest coach in collegiate football history, once shared a story about the transition in his leadership approach. Nick briefly explains to a group of colleagues on television that, in the early stages of his coaching career, he functioned primarily as a transactional leader. His concern was limited strictly to results. When things went well for his team and coaching staff, he would acknowledge their efforts and celebrate them. Conversely, when things went poorly, he would criticise them and recognised that when he criticised without providing guidance, his actions impacted morale.[2]

He goes on to mention that in the late nineties, while coaching at Michigan State with a record of 4-5 and an upcoming game against the number one team in the nation, Ohio State, he wasn't too confident in their ability to win.[2] After doing some soul searching, he decided to focus less on the result of the game and more on the process that leads to the results of the game. He set a clear vision of what he believed his team could achieve collectively. He modelled a person that others could emulate, and he genuinely became concerned about the benefit of others over himself.[2] From this posture of servitude, his team entered the game with a newfound confidence in their ability, and they played beyond expectations and won the game. Nick's eyes were opened as a leader in that moment, and his entire coaching philosophy shifted from there.

From Small Steps to Big Leaps

When I was a teenager, I can remember my father taking me to learn how to drive. It was a rainy day, and we were in a van that he had to move some items for work. We had been discussing this moment for a long time, and I was eager to get behind the wheel for the first time. I had taken my written test, been granted a permit, and thought I was ready to drive on my own. In my ignorance of the law, I learned that I needed a licensed driver in the vehicle with me, and I still had much to learn.

Early Saturday morning, we woke up, got dressed and had breakfast. As I'm eating my cereal, I can't stop thinking about how well this is going to work out. In my head, I was having a conversation in which I declared that I was the greatest driver in the world and that I would pick up driving fundamentals quickly. After all I had seen both my mother and father drive several times, and I had gained insight into what I could do, and I couldn't. What I was unaware of was the vast difference between the concept and the reality of controlling a several-thousand-pound cargo van in the rain. But this was going to go great, right?

Fast forward, I'm behind the wheel with my father on my right, spotting everything ahead of me and calling out directions as I drive. My confidence was through the roof as we did k-turns, parallel parked, and a few other things. All was going well until it was time to head back home. I allowed my early success to dictate my actions, and I let my focus slip for a moment. In that moment, in the rain, as we were heading back home through the suburban streets, I not only ran a stop sign but also hit the curb and almost crashed into another vehicle, out of pure shock.

This was a significant change in my life that could very well be considered transformational, but I neglected to give the moment the respect it deserved. Eventually, I regained my confidence, but I delayed obtaining my license for several years because of that incident. I learned then that fast and first doesn't always mean good. The quality of something is not based solely on speed; there are many additional factors to consider. As we think about what it takes to become a transformational leader, overcoming the fear of personal transformation is the beginning of the journey for most of us.

Dr J. Robert Clinton wrote a book entitled The Making of a Leader. In his book, Clinton explores the idea that leaders need a roadmap of recognition to avoid making decisions in haste and without recognising long-range development in their lives.[3] This roadmap includes the phases the leader encounters throughout their development. Why is this important for us to know? I have heard the myths that leaders are born, not made, and that good leadership can happen overnight, even though every good leader has been through a process.

When I say 'good,' let me first define good leadership. In brevity, these are leaders who have taken the time to identify their values, identity, and skill set, with the intention of leveraging them to serve humanity. These are selfless leaders, not self-serving leaders. Leaders who desire to make an impact in other people's lives, not just drive people for results. In this world, good results are a by-product of how these individuals treat others and not the primary focus.

Clinton's first two phases include sovereign foundations and inner-life growth.[3] Essentially, what do you believe and value, and how will you change to mature into the leader necessary for the time you are in? When I first drove that cargo van, I was talented, confident, and astute. The flip side of that was that I was also arrogant, undisciplined, and unsure of myself. Every leader, as McIntosh & Rima reference, has a dark side to overcome.[4] Hearing this should be taken with excitement, not guilt. What it shows is how you function today as a leader, if you're honest with yourself, it may not be how you need to function tomorrow if you're looking to create sustainable success.

As I mentioned earlier, eventually I was able to drive that cargo van and, after that, truly anything with four wheels. I had come to understand that my internal motivation was just as important, if not more important, than my outward expression as a leader. I also learned that leadership wasn't a role I was trying to function in, but a life I was building.

The Leaders GPS

> *Is your ego larger than your purpose?*

Technology has advanced significantly over the last 60 years. From the first Apple computer in 1976 to cell phones, Google, and the rise of social media. Most recently, artificial intelligence has begun to make a name for itself. With all these changes, there is no telling what will happen next, flying cars? Of all these inventions and technological breakthroughs, one has given me a level of comfort and ease unlike others. The global positioning system, or GPS, has revolutionized how people travel and reach their destinations.

The Waze app provides real-time updates on crashes, traffic, and alternate routes, and even alerts you to where hidden police officers are stationed, waiting for someone to exceed the speed limit. The GPS is not only a roadmap; its intuitive live updates position it as a guide on the road. If you were to visit a foreign country with only a map, you would have the directions only to get to your destination. But if you had a guide, you would understand the terrain along the way and remain agile enough to get to your destination despite the obstacles ahead.

Many leaders believe their style or individual perspective on how to lead is correct, and if they have achieved proven success, it becomes even more challenging to influence them to see things differently. So why would a leader need a GPS? The greatest leaders throughout history all shared a willingness to learn from others. Regardless of the level of influence, vision, or mystique they walked with underneath it all, they knew they could not and should not attempt to lead on their own. Simon Sinek calls leadership a team sport, where the different parts are interdependent.[5]

In our own stubbornness and unwillingness to change, we can easily find ourselves believing we are leading a group of people when we are, in fact, alone, walking by ourselves. It takes courage to recognize this internally and bravery to execute. Is your ego larger than your purpose? If it is, unfortunately, it is more likely you will become a leader others despise, and they will respond to you out of fear, not respect. But if you are willing to leverage your leadership GPS and locate yourself before you begin this journey towards transformation, I look forward to seeing the next version of you on the other side.

Reflect: The Mirror of Self and Mission

Leadership begins within. Reflection is the daily discipline that helps us align who we are with who we want to become. In life and community, this reflection is deeply personal; it's about character, calling, and consistency.

Practical Applications:

- Personal Journaling - end each day with one reflection.

- Community discussions where participants share lessons from personal challenges

- Faith or civic groups use reflection circles to assess how collective values align with action.

Inspire: Story as a Source of Strength

Inspiration in community leadership comes from authenticity when people see that your story has been shaped by struggle and anchored in purpose. We all have a story, but few realize the power it holds to encourage others.

Practical Applications:
- Host community story nights where residents share lessons of resilience and hope
- Parents and mentors share personal stories of failure and faith with youth.
- Use digital storytelling - blogs, podcasts, or social media to highlight everyday heroes.

Serve: The Heartbeat of Community Leadership

Service is what connects personal reflection to collective impact. When we serve, we strengthen the bonds of belonging. Service leadership is not about doing everything for others; it's about helping others see that they can do something too.

Practical Applications:
- Volunteer at local youth programs or mentorship initiatives
- Support community cleanup or service projects with your family or team.
- Offer your professional skills (finance, leadership, communication) as pro bono mentorship for small businesses or nonprofits.

Elevate: From Individual Growth to Collective Legacy

Elevation happens when we invest in others so deeply that our impact continues through them. When individuals elevate others through mentoring, sponsorship or community building, they multiply influence and sustain progress.

Practical Applications:

- Create intergenerational mentoring programs connecting professionals with students.

- Recognize and celebrate community members who model R.I.S.E. principles.

Consider Eunice Hunton Carter once more; her story did not end with her. Her commitment to justice elevated generations of women and leaders who followed in her footsteps. Similarly, in every town and classroom, there are leaders whose quiet courage shapes the culture of tomorrow. Leadership that elevates doesn't always make headlines; it makes history. When leadership leaves the boardroom and enters the living room, transformation begins. The R.I.S.E. framework isn't just a model for organizational success; it's a manual for human flourishing. If we reflect with honesty, inspire with purpose, serve with humility, and elevate with intention, we won't just change our communities, we'll change generations.

---

1. Hendricks, G. (2009). The Big Leap. HarperCollins Publishers.

2. Nick Saban. (2024, Oct 5). On being a 'Transformational Leader' + Cal film room breakdown | College GameDay [Video]. YouTube. https://youtu.be/OJqtnawj7fA?si=ni5yGk-C1ahemHjT

3. Clinton, J.R. (2012). The Making of a Leader 2nd edition: Recognizing the lessons and stages of leadership development. Tyndale House Publishers, Inc.

4. McIntosh, G.L., & Rima, S.D. (2008). Overcoming the Dark Side of Leadership. Baker Books.

5. Sinek, S. (2024, Jan). Leadership is a Team Sport: [Video] Simon Sinek

Part III – Your Rise

CHAPTER 9

The Commitment to Rise: Living the Framework

"Creativity is contagious, pass it on".

Albert Einstein

TRANSFORMATION DOES NOT BEGIN with opportunity; it begins with commitment. Every leader reaches a moment when belief must become behavior and when knowing must become doing. This chapter is that moment. To commit to R.I.S.E. means to live intentionally, to lead from values, and to pursue growth that benefits others as much as it benefits yourself. Your rise is not measured by how far you climb, but by how many you bring with you.

One of the distinguishing factors of true transformational leadership is the standing influence the individual has when they are no longer present. Legacy speaks to lasting impact, and these types of leaders are meticulous in their actions because they not only see the challenge they face currently but also consider the evolution of challenges in the future. They have an outlook and perspective unique to the time they are in.

While watching a movie, oddly enough entitled Transformers One, there is a scene where two of the transformers are having a conversation about leadership. The female transformer tells the main character that he carries a blind optimism, leading him to hope in situations that are hopeless. She emphasized this as she encouraged him to lean into his instincts that she believed qualified him for leadership. His ability to see beyond the present and articulate an influential vision of the future resembles the life of Alvin Ailey.

Challenging Beginnings

Alvin Ailey is known for revolutionizing modern dance through his creative and innovative expression. His life is synonymous with risk-taking, challenging the status quo, and breaking barriers. He lived a life of impact and external transformation because he himself had experienced internal transformation. When we look at our own stories and reflect on the moments when we feel inadequate, we need to acknowledge that many individuals throughout history have made substantial changes that began in obscurity.

Alvin was born in the 1930s when public segregation was commonplace.[1] The feeling of being considered less than human for young Alvin was not helped when, three months after his birth, his father left him and his mother to fend for themselves. Alvin Sr. lacked the discipline and work ethic necessary to lead a family and raise a son, so the burden fell to his mother, Lula, who accepted this role with poise and grace.[2] She was determined to ensure young Alvin would have a chance to become something.

Lula would do anything for her son, which included, at one point, walking eight miles in the middle of the night to take him to a doctor who would see black children.[1] The amount of danger on that path wasn't a hindrance for Lula, although she was keenly aware of the risk. This trip resulted in a change in her living and work situation. Coincidentally, after Lula and her son were in a better financial position, Alvin Sr. returned to re-establish his presence as a husband and father. Lula recognized her true motives and, four months later, took Alvin Jr. away from his father with the hope of a better future.[1]

It appears that Alvin Jr.'s optimism would have come directly from his mother. However, Alvin and Lula still had challenges to overcome. The pressure of being the sole provider for the family wore heavily on Lula and resulted in alcoholism. One scenario that would be a marker for Alvin Jr. was when Lula came across an advertisement for a job in a larger town, which she took by dropping off her son with her sister for three weeks. When she returned, Alvin informed her that while he was with the other children, they experimented sexually with each other.[1] Why is this part of Alvin's story relevant? Every transformational leader has experiences that shape the trajectory of their own transformation, leading to the opportunity to transform others.

As Alvin grew older, his curiosity about the arts was piqued after he avoided more competitive sports like baseball and football out of fear of injury.[1] As a teenager, Alvin was exposed to the Horton Dance Theater in Los Angeles, where all the arts and opportunity for creative expression became a playground and university for him.[1] His hunger to learn was infectious, and his desire for perfection accentuated his level of discipline. Alvin would become a trendsetter, an inspiration, and an open door to opportunity for many people of color throughout his career.

Will You Lead?

> *If you're not willing to be challenged as a leader, then you are not ready for leadership.*

Kouzes & Posner emphasize that one of the practices of sound leadership is the ability to inspire through a shared vision.[3] A subset of that practice is to enlist others through appealing to common ideals and animating the vision.[3] Alvin was committed to empowering his dancers and collaborators to express themselves fully on and off stage. He recognized from his own story that when people are given clear direction and an opportunity to perform, with the right support system, they can learn to fly. Because of this, Alvin intentionally connected to what was meaningful to his dancers and created a space of inclusion in the industry regardless of what was happening at the societal level.

We all have dreams and aspirations, but transformational leaders awaken and breathe life into those dreams within others by pointing them towards purposeful activity.[4] Activity with a purpose means efficiency and the removal of waste. For a budding leader, this can easily be taken out of context and misunderstood if not handled appropriately. If you're not willing to be challenged as a leader, then you are not ready for leadership. The idea that what I say goes as the leader is not only outdated but also highly ineffective.

Studies show that organizational diversity leads to higher profit margins.[5] This also includes diversity of thought in the rooms where innovative conversations take place. If the only people we surround ourselves with are those who see things the same way we do, then who accounts for our blind spots? Perhaps you are, or have been, in a situation where your perspective was different from others in the room, but, out of fear, you hesitated to share your insight. These situations are not about who is right or wrong; they are opportunities to arrive at a place that has been pressure-tested across different purviews.

The question you lead is a call to all of us, whether we have a title, a degree, or formal authority. Feedback is free, and the only cost is when we don't share it; we rob people of opportunities for growth. Kouzes & Posner believe leadership is never about you alone, but about you and your constituents.[6] Yes, there will be moments that require swift, decisive action, and the leader's perspective at that time will be most poignant, but the transformational leader is an exceptional listener who processes decisions, accounting for future impact.

Fresh Vision

Alvin Ailey was not ignorant of the social injustice of his day, nor was he naïve to the impact those challenges had on his community. Like Optimus Prime in Transformers One, Alvin had visionary creativity. Specifically, he drew on African American cultural experience and integrated it with modern dance, with the intent not only to create entertainment but also to produce social change.[2] Later in his life, he would find the Alvin Ailey American Dance Theater, where he would develop a space for underrepresented groups to get the training and opportunity to creatively express themselves through the medium of dance.[2]

As Alvin essentially risked everything, including his company, his career, and his reputation to provide a voice to the voiceless, he embodied the impact transformational leaders are called to have. By stepping out of the confines of how dance was expressed to that point, he created a new lane where racial and social barriers could be broken, and the focus could be not the color of someone's skin alone, but their skill set on display.

The Extra Mile

In previous generations, it was common for someone to remain at an establishment for an extended period. There was a level of commitment from the employee and the employer that is not as tangible today as it once was. What happened? Technology has opened the door to accelerated growth in every aspect of business. Globalism has changed the market, giving business owners additional opportunities to consider and competitors to prepare for. The result has been a flood of innovation, with startups, small businesses, and unicorns changing the way everyone does business.

Why is this important? Companies today are having to keep pace with the rate of change, which is causing employers' commitments to shift. The expectation in the workplace today is for both employees and employers to operate with agility and be prepared to change course in response to business needs, which can happen at any moment. Indirectly, this has brought instability and unpredictability to the workforce that previous generations were accustomed to. So now, when an organization gives someone a job description on day one, there is an unspoken expectation that they will go beyond the scope of the role as defined on paper.

Here lies the disconnect between employee and employer. The "what's in it for me" (*WIFM*) has not been made clear to the employee resulting in a less incentivized and engaged workforce. "What's in it for me?" is the question employees are asking more frequently today as they realize technology has created more opportunities for them to explore than before. The consciousness of the workforce today is different from what it was historically, meaning the organizations that are aware enough to adjust with the times will find success, and the others will continue to struggle.

Transformational leaders are not only aware of this hurdle, but they can function above it. Bass & Riggio suggest that these leaders boost followers' self-concept while encouraging them to see themselves within the group's overarching goals and objectives.[7] By doing this, they help the individual self-identify with something larger than themselves, accomplishing a win-win scenario for the leader and follower. The leader gets the support necessary to accomplish the goal, and the follower gets the opportunity to step outside of their own limitations, simultaneously increasing their individual skill set and fulfilling an objective in the larger picture.

How To Function

The leader accomplishes these things by leveraging aspects of transformational leadership tailored to the audience being impacted. These components include the following:

Idealized Influence – **Reflection**

Inspirational Motivation - **Inspiration**

Intellectual Stimulation – **Serve**

Individualized Consideration - **Elevate**

The motivation from a transformational leader is unique in that it is expressed through the leader's ability to provide meaning and challenge to the follower's actions. This can simply be the articulation of a clear vision that is explicit enough for the follower to see where they fit. If it is unclear, the transformational leader can direct the follower by involving them in creating a compelling future state.

Kouzes & Posner suggest people have an innate desire to make a difference and engage in something meaningful and important.[6] Transformational leaders acknowledge hidden potential in others well because they have their own experience to pull from. They realize that a shared vision has greater reach than an isolated one. Alvin exemplifies this through the standard he created in the performing arts industry. His commitment to growth and emphasis on inclusion have enabled his institution to influence future generations of dancers and leaders.

Leaders often understand their why early and often. It is the why that drives them to pursue challenges, identify solutions, and impact people along the way. What can get lost in the mix is the how. The tactical execution of transformational leadership doesn't come in a microwave. There is a process, and the sooner the leader recognizes this, the better off they will be. Consider the Chinese bamboo tree. It grows underground for the first five years as a seed, expanding its roots. Five years come and go, and on the surface, there is no tangible change, no growth, and seemingly no progress to report. However, after those five years, in the sixth year, within the first five weeks, that same tree will grow over ninety feet tall. The how behind a leader matters.

Establishing Credibility

Leadership differs from management. Grace Murray Hopper says, "You *manage things; you lead people.*" We have all experienced poor leadership at some point. Whether we were the observer or the initiator, we can remember what we felt during those moments. Johnson & Hackman believe leadership is not limited to how you act, but what you do, how you do it, and who you are.[8] True leadership recognizes it cannot lead effectively from a false perspective.

How can I bring someone to a place that I have not been before effectively? Sure, prior experiences have prepared the leader for a journey into the unknown, but without context, this road would be challenging. Senior leaders join organizations or individuals are promoted into roles where they feel almost immediate pressure to perform. Perhaps the organization is in a very challenging moment, and the expectation is that you will quickly turn things around.

Change is not instant, and lasting change takes time. Kouzes & Posner conducted extensive research, surveying thousands of managers nationwide, to identify the key characteristics of leaders they admire.[9] The hypothesis was that admired leaders are followed because people vote with their actions, not their words. What they found was a consensus around three characteristics: honesty, competence, and inspiring.[9] These same characteristics also happen to be the three factors that researchers refer to as source credibility.[9]

Therefore, credibility is what leadership is built upon. People ask themselves: can this person inspire me, does this person have a track record of accomplishing what they say, and does this leader have the competence needed for this task? If the answer to these questions is yes, then the leader has an opportunity to earn commitment.[9] Even then, credibility is earned through every 1:1 interaction; it's earned through intimate moments where leaders are seen as people and not only positions.[9]

Transformational Journey

Along the journey to becoming a transformational leader, building your credibility is critical. Focus groups, conversations, and asking questions all help you identify the current state, providing a baseline to imagine the future and determine priorities to get there.

Another form of credibility that does not get as much fanfare is humility. Often humility is seen as weakness, especially in leadership circles, but it is a significant strength if harnessed correctly.

Imagine the assembly of a team with a leader walking with humility. They do not see themselves above anyone else, which gives them access to others' knowledge and insights that would otherwise hold them back from expressing their opinions for fear of being unheard. When someone is humble, it does not mean they do not recognize the value they bring; rather, they are open to the value in others and look for ways to highlight it.

In a time where inclusion can be interpreted differently depending on who you speak with, a leader has the responsibility to build a safe environment where others can be heard, seen, and accepted. Of the many accomplishments Alvin Ailey had throughout his life, his ability to create space for others is what made him transformational. Will you be the type of leader who acknowledges or overlooks others? Your foundation as a leader resides in the answer to this question. Transformation is not reserved for the extraordinary. It belongs to those willing to grow, to choose courage over comfort, and to purpose over position. The question is not whether you can rise, it's whether you will.

Reflect: Begin With Awareness

Reflection grounds the journey. Before you can lead others, you must first understand your purpose, patterns, and potential. Leadership begins when you have the courage to look inward.

Practical Application:
- Conduct a Personal Values Audit: list your top five values and ask, "Where are these visible in my daily decisions?"

- Write a one-sentence Leadership Purpose Statement.

- Schedule a recurring time for reflection - 15 minutes at the end of each week to assess growth.

True reflection is where transformation begins and where arrogance ends.

Inspire: Lead With Vision

Every meaningful movement begins with a story. When you articulate what you believe and why it matters, you inspire others to act. Your story can move people more than your strategy ever will.

Practical Application:

- Write your Leadership Story: a short narrative of what shaped your values and purpose.

- Share that story with someone who looks to you for guidance.

- Use storytelling in your workplace, classroom, or home to communicate hope and possibility.

People don't follow titles; they follow authenticity and belief.

Serve: Lead By Lifting Others

Commitment is tested in how we treat people. Service isn't a soft skill; it's a spiritual discipline of humility and honor. When you lead to serve, you align your power with purpose.

Practical Application:

- Identify one person you can intentionally mentor or encourage this month.

- Ask your team or family: "What can I do to support you

better?"

- Engage in an act of service that stretches your comfort zone.

The leaders who serve are remembered long after the leaders who rule.

Elevate: Multiply Your Impact

The true sign of leadership maturity is not personal achievement but generational continuity. To elevate means to empower others to lead, to build systems, relationships, and cultures that thrive beyond your presence.

Practical Application:

- Build an Elevation Plan: List three people you can equip to take greater responsibility.

- Create a RISE Circle - A small group dedicated to practicing and discussing leadership growth.

- Document your leadership process so others can replicate your impact.

Elevation transforms leadership from momentary success to lasting legacy.

---

1. Dunning, J. (1998). Alvin Ailey A Life In Dance. Da Capo Press.

2. Ailey, A. (1995). Revelations. The Autobiography of Alvin Ailey. Carol Publishing Group.

3. Kouzes, J.M., & Posner, B.Z. (2017). The Leadership Challenge 6th edition. John Wiley & Sons, Inc.

4. Burns, J.M. (2003). Transforming Leadership. Grove Press.

5. Dixon-Fyle, S., Hunt, V, Huber, C., Martinez Marquez, M. del M., Prince, S., & Thomas, A. (2023). Diversity Matters Even More: The Case For Holistic Impact. https://www.mckinsey.com/featured-insights/diversity-and-inclusion/diversity-matters-even-more-the-case-for-holistic-impact .

6. Kouzes, J.M., & Posner, B.Z. (2010). The Truth About Leadership. John Wiley & Sons, Inc.

7. Bass, B.M., & Riggio, R.E. (2014). Transformational Leadership 2nd edition. Routledge.

8. Johnson, C.E., & Hackman, M.Z. (2018). Leadership. A Communication Perspective 7th Edition. Waveland Press, Inc.

9. Kouzes, J.M., & Posner, B.Z. (2011). Credibility: How leaders gain and lose it why people demand it. John Wiley & Sons, Inc.

CHAPTER 10

Beyond The Climb

"What lies behind us and what lies before us are tiny matters compared to what lies within us."
Oliver Wendell Holmes

MY WIFE HAS AN eye for interior decoration. From the day we returned to our three-bedroom apartment after our honeymoon to the purchase of our first home right before the pandemic, she has displayed the ability to see an empty room as though it had been filled with furnishings, color, flooring, you name it. While we were looking for our first home, we found ourselves watching a lot of HGTV, indulging ourselves in the latest shows featuring current trends and advice to consider for ourselves. While I was personally more concerned with the home's price than my wife, her eye for detail would prove a guiding light for us in our decision-making.

She considered the items in a home we were both were looking for and identified a list of priorities for us to begin our search. It was an arduous process, marked by plenty of disappointment, frustration, and, at times, even anger, but eventually we found our home. It was a nice size in an area that was child-friendly, with a private school system we believed would provide our children with the type of education they would benefit from. As we signed the pile of papers to conclude the selling process, I realized we had an uphill journey ahead of us. Here we were with the keys to begin a future together in an environment where our children would have the space and freedom to play, learn, be loud, and grow. It was at this point that I realized the principle that says all things are created twice came alive for me.[1] In Steven Covey's book, The 7 Habits of Highly Effective People, he makes the statement "Begin with the end in mind," which resonated with me when I first heard it and has had a profound impact on the way I function today.[1]

My wife, in that moment, had already created the inner workings of our home before we began a series of trips to Home Goods, Ikea, Wayfair, and more. What's interesting about beginning with the end in mind is that there is no limit to where it can be applied. In business, teams formulate strategies with an expected end in mind. When a professor is teaching a course, they consider the result and build backwards. In every example I could list, there is a blueprint for a plan before it is executed. So why do we think the development of a leader is any different? There is the inner construction before the outward structure.

Leadership Is An Inside Job

A transformational leader, globally known as an international diplomat who counseled kings and political leaders, was Myles Munroe. Dr. Munroe wore many hats, including Pastor, Author, Father, Counselor & friend. Of all the hats he wore, many would say he was best known for developing leaders and for his pursuit of understanding leadership. In one of his books, The Spirit of

Leadership, Dr. Munroe offers his personal definition of leadership, which reinforces the idea that leadership begins internally and is expressed externally. Dr. Munroe says, "Leadership *is* the capacity to influence others through inspiration motivated by a passion, generated by a vision, produced by a conviction, ignited by a purpose."[2] The keyword here is purpose.

Dr. Munroe believed that, at the core of leadership is a fire ignited by purpose. The question "What is my purpose?" is searched for over 5,000 times per month, according to Google Trends.[3] To think that people want to know the answer to this question would be an understatement. So where does leadership fit into this equation? Whether someone is extrinsically or intrinsically motivated to lead, there is an inner drive that propels them forward. Consider if I want to make a lot of money, and that is my external motivation, I will still need to do my due diligence as an individual to position myself for the opportunity to be a high earner. The journey still begins inside.

One of the challenges we face in our quest to become transformational leaders is denial. McIntosh & Rima believe denial is akin to a deadly disease that every leader should be infused.[4] While I would not go so far as to agree with this statement, I see the fine line of validity available. Often, leaders find themselves in situations where they believe they must live up to a certain standard to gain credibility and respect. While this may be true, it does not tell the entire story. Leaders are self-aware, recognize they do not have all the answers, and show a willingness to learn and change. This can be balanced with knowing when to exercise discretion to avoid discrediting yourself. Northouse suggests that authenticity in leadership comes from a leader's self-knowledge, self-regulation, and self-concept.[5] Notice in this example there is an internal pursuit before and outward expression.

Why is a focus on the internal aspects of leadership so important to the transformational leader? Imagine an influential leader whom you admire. Do you know their personal story, or are you more aware of their expression and accomplishments? These are questions for you to consider, but your answers are confidential. When we catch glimpses of these influential figures' lives without understanding the full context of their backgrounds, we can easily focus on the results rather than the process. This is the equivalent of seeing a butterfly in flight, functioning in its purpose. The variety of colors and designs is intriguing and gives us an opportunity to pause and see their beauty as they pass by. Would we have the same response to the worm moving slowly and carefully as it attempts to avoid becoming a casualty of nature? My guess is we would not be as interested, at least initially.

How Do You See Yourself?

> *Your projection is your **protection**.*

When you wake up in the morning and look in the mirror before you begin your day, what do you see? The mirror gives you a reflection of yourself visually that your eyes help interpret. But that is not the only reflection happening in that moment. Outwardly, you may see yourself one way, but inwardly, your interpretation may be contradictory. The book of Proverbs tells us, *"As he thinks in his heart, so is he."*[6] This means we are who we believe we are. If I see myself as a confident, prepared transformational leader, my outward challenges cannot impact my belief. This is important because, as a leader your *projection is your protection.* In moments when transformational leadership is required, it is usually because other methods do not meet the objective or deliver the results needed for sustainable success. The transformational leader will often find themselves in highly challenging situations and will feel as though they are swimming against the current. Why the resistance? Because transformation is messy, tough, and requires grit, agility, and commitment. During that process, there may arise moments of weakness, doubt, and unbelief, which is when our internal picture becomes critical. How we see ourselves shapes our mindset, which in turn shapes our decisions, which in turn shapes our credibility and influence. The transformational leader's ability to see when no one else sees protects them from the onslaught of opposition as it comes. Notice I said 'protect'; I did not say 'remove'.

The ability to remain steadfast in the hurricane is a mindset and skill that underpins the transformational leader.[7] Seeing yourself as a title that qualifies you to lead only is a detriment to your true leadership potential. Maxwell refers to positional leadership as a lonely place where you get branded and stranded.[8] Leaders who rely on position for influence focus on control rather than contribution, which produces followers who feel undervalued and stagnant.[8] If we are to create real change, then real change needs to be alive and well inside of us.

Be A Difference Maker

Mayberry suggests that transformational leaders are making a difference long before being given a title, and they are not concerned with how others view them because they have an inherent motivation to build up those around them.[7] Leadership is something that is earned, not given. I remember working for a Fortune 500 company and being put into a precarious situation. Four managers were hired to oversee an operational team of approximately 500 people, with primary responsibility given to only three, while one manager was to provide supplemental support as needed. Guess who was the odd person out? Me, of course. I was the most tenured, most experienced, and most prepared for this opportunity, but I was essentially placed on the sidelines. So, the inward journey of transformational leadership began.

Was I initially discouraged, of course. Briefly, I felt as though I had made the wrong decision to join such a prestigious organization, and I became concerned with things that were out of my control, which left me filled with anxiety and fear. Once I got past this moment, I began looking inward at what I could influence directly. I began to question how I show up despite the contradictory circumstances. This led to realignment with my values as a leader and to the recognition that my purpose was not defined by a title but by my actions. So, I began to express a level of curiosity I wasn't aware I had. My conversations spanned across teams, functions, authority levels, and industries. I began to identify gaps in our processes, learning, and standards, which opened the door to implementing changes I had identified as impactful from my time in discovery.

As my time at this organization continued, I was influencing the entire function without being given formal authority over a particular group of people. It was uncomfortable but transformational. Eventually, one of the other managers was terminated for subpar performance, and I was given oversight of more than half of the five hundred-plus team. The relationships I was able to foster and the solutions we identified and implemented had a significant impact on our revenue generation, attrition rates, leadership pipeline, and scalable processes across a 10,000-plus-member organization. Why am I sharing this with you? Because how we see ourselves directly impacts how we will lead. Instead of remaining in a victim mindset, I chose to challenge myself, which led me to challenge others to be more than what we believed we were. This is not magic, nor is it strictly conceptual. It is a practical application of the transformational leadership model. Each of us has the unique opportunity and potential to become transformational leaders. Always remember that the situation reveals the leader, but the leader impacts the situation.

Take Ownership Of Your Story

The power of a coach in a leader's life is significant. I have been fortunate enough to receive executive-level coaching, and one question I have always been asked is, knowing what I know now, what would I have done differently and why? These questions always place me in a posture of deep reflection as I analyze the good, the bad, and the ugly of my decisions. The open-ended questions give me space to identify and embrace my entire story without fear of judgment. The same principle applies to our own history. Each of us has a unique past that, if viewed with a critical eye, could offer lessons that not only impact us but also others today and in the future.

For us to own our story we first must leverage it to empower our individual journeys. Meaning taking our past experiences and reframing them as learning opportunities. By doing this, we open the door to transparency that leaders need to influence others. Another part of owning our stories includes probing beyond the surface of our failures to uncover the unmet needs those experiences left us with.[9] When we identify those emotional triggers, we can move past the self-imposed behaviors that limit transformational potential, such as the need to fulfill expectations imposed on us by others.[9] A leader must be free from the people they lead in order to be effective. But if they concern themselves with being liked, seeking approval, or the need for friendship, they will be unable to fulfill their transformational assignment.

Embrace The Ongoing Journey Of Transformation

James Kouzes and Barry Posner are two highly influential researchers, professors, scholars, and advocates of leadership. They have been studying leaders worldwide for well over 40 years and have interviewed thousands of individuals across a variety of sectors to support their conclusions. In The Leadership Challenge, Kouzes & Posner state that there is no research indicating that leaders are required to be perfect.[10] Isn't that comforting to hear? The research does just the opposite, in fact showing us the strengths and flaws in our leaders historically. Statements such as "learn to fail forward" take on deeper meaning when we recognize we are a work in progress.

The path of transformational leadership is filled with challenges. Northouse notes that the transformational leadership style has been seen as elitist and viewed with hero bias by many who challenge its effectiveness.[5] However, at the core of the transformational leader is an individual no longer concerned about fulfilling the status quo assignment or leading followers with predictability. Instead, these leaders welcome the difficulty and education that becoming this type of leader brings.

---

1. Covey, S. R. (1990). The 7 Habits of Highly Effective People. Irving Perkins Associates.

2. Munroe, M. (2005). The Spirit of Leadership. Munroe Group of Companies LTD.

3. What is my Purpose: Google. (2024). Google Trends. Retrieved [Nov 11, 2024], from https://trends.google.com/trends/explore

4. McIntosh, G.L., & Rima, S.D. (2008). Overcoming the Dark Side of Leadership. Baker Books.

5. Northouse, P.G. (2021). Leadership Theory & Practice 9th edition. SAGE Publications, Inc.

6. The Holy Bible, New King James Version. (1982). Thomas, Nelson, Inc.

7. Mayberry, M. (2024). The Transformational Leader: How the world's best leaders build teams, inspire action, and achieve lasting success. John Wiley & Sons, Inc.

8. Maxwell, J.C. (2011). The 5 Levels of Leadership. Hachette Book Group.

9. Kouzes, J.M., & Posner, B.Z. (2010). The Truth About Leadership. John Wiley & Sons, Inc.

10. Kouzes, J.M., & Posner, B.Z. (2017). The Leadership Challenge 6th edition. John Wiley & Sons, Inc.

Chapter 11

A Rising Generation: The Future of Leadership

> "And do not be conformed to this world, but be transformed by the renewing of your mind, that you may prove what is that good and acceptable and perfect will of God."
>
> Romans 12:2 NKJV

THE FINAL STAGE OF R.I.S.E. is not about personal fulfillment but collective movement. As we close this book, we look ahead to a generation of leaders who are self-aware, empathetic, service-driven, and legacy-minded. These are not just leaders of tomorrow; they are influencers of today.

Mentorship in many areas can accelerate someone's life in ways experience cannot. Why? Imagine walking down a street with potholes, patches of ice, and many other dangerous hazards with limited visibility, oh, and did I mention this is in the dark? This would be a challenging walk to your destination. Now take that same route and insert the insights from someone who has already gone ahead and charted this path before you. Do you see the amount of insight they could provide you? The guidance rooted in experience that they would be able to pass down to you. By leveraging these relationships for growth and learning they have the possibility to influence the trajectory of someone's life. Why would we be willing to listen attentively to these individuals?

The answer is simple. We can see the tangible difference in their lifestyle, actions, accomplishments, and any other descriptive word you want to consider. The Bible positions this in Matthew 7:20, where the writer says, "Therefore by their fruits you will know them."[1] The context behind this is Jesus drawing a distinction between those who know him and those who do not. He paints a picture of a tree and discusses the differences between good and bad trees, grapes and thorns, and the fruit they bear. The heart of the matter is that who we are on the inside eventually is revealed in what we produce on the outside. There are countless scriptures that highlight this principle, including ... to name a few. I believe the same principle applies to the transformational leader. How can one be an effective transformational agent if they themselves have not experienced the rigor of transformation? It would be challenging for someone to teach others to sell something without having done so themselves.

A Life Transformed

The common thread is that every transformational leader has experienced personal transformation first, which enabled and empowered them to become the leaders necessary to drive impactful historical change. Transformation exists at the core of who I am and influences everything that I do and will do in the future. My childhood was filled with confusion, anger, and a lack of emotional stability, which caused me to question my identity, purpose, and ability. When you're not given a roadmap or provided with clear direction, it's easy to try, fail, try something else, fail, and keep the cycle going again and again. Many of us are here now or have been in this place of repetition, feeling that progress was impossible.

What this does is keep us in a state of paralysis, without the opportunity to fulfill our purpose. Transformational leaders are not only influential but necessary. I met one when I was in college, attending a school over six hours from my hometown with a female-to-male ratio of eighteen to one. I was highly distracted and failing to fulfill my responsibilities as a student. During this time, I was placed on academic probation twice while carrying a .06 GPA and eventually kicked out of school. I remember attending a BBQ early that summer back in my hometown and being challenged by a friend from high school. He may not have realized it, but his words caused me to look at my life with sobriety in that moment. He asked me why I was back home instead of in school, and my answer wasn't sufficient. He then told me directly that there was more in me and that I needed to do whatever I could to continue my education. I laughed it off in front of everyone at the BBQ, but I took those words to heart and made some changes.

Fast forward: after working three jobs and saving enough to get back into school without financial aid, I returned to school, but my motivation dwindled just as quickly as it had accelerated to get me there. My advisor noticed this internal struggle within me on campus. Internally, I wanted to be there and perform well, but externally, I was struggling, lacking focus and discipline. Eventually, my advisor pulled me aside after class one day and spoke with me She asked me what I wanted to do with myself. Up to that point in my nineteen years, I had been asked this question before, but for some reason, hearing it in that moment had a different effect on me. It was as if her words felt like a siren that resounded within me, awakening something inside me that I didn't know existed.

I answered her with trepidation and transparency, saying I had no idea about my future or what I wanted to do or become. I realized at that moment that I didn't have a clear blueprint for my life. My advisor paused and, with a smirk, told me her plan. It involved naming me the Vice President of a student organization focused on empowering minorities in hospitality through education, exposure, and experience. The responsibilities would entail leading a department of students to maximize learning opportunities while at school. Immediately, I told her how inadequate and underprepared I felt to take on this assignment, and she completely disregarded my excuses. What I didn't realize in that moment was that all I needed was an opportunity.

This was the beginning of my personal transformation. At the same time, I had a tangible, permanent, and life-changing experience with Jesus outside of church. My outlook on life began to shift, and I realized that my actions had a purpose. Lorrits suggests leaders are not defined by the positions they occupy, but by the assignments they have been given and the contributions they make.[2] From that moment, I realized I had been given the opportunity to lead not for selfish ambition or personal gain, but to serve others. My grades began to change rapidly, my confidence grew, and the impact I had on people became clear. It was an organic change that led me to come home the following summer break with a hunger to learn unlike I had ever had before.

This transformation inside of me has been and will continue to be an ongoing process that I have fully embraced. As I graduated and continued to grow in my life and career, I began to witness transformations happening beyond me. The workplace became a training ground for me to learn how to execute transformational leadership. There were countless moments I remember that reinforce the notion that leadership is a privilege and should not be approached haphazardly. I will share a couple of examples to provide practical context for what this may look like.

Transformation in Practice

While serving as the general manager of a quick-service restaurant chain, I had the opportunity to build a team, open a new location, and train two other general managers. What a unique situation. Our thoughts on leadership were vastly different, and our perspectives added diversity that ultimately proved beneficial. But make no mistake, this was challenging terrain to navigate. During this time, my team was learning, growing, and being challenged by other leaders and me to become the best versions of themselves.

I held regular check-ins with every employee, giving me the opportunity to connect deeply with them and understand their strengths, weaknesses, and motivators. As our restaurant continued to gain exposure and stability, our influence in the community grew, attracting more customers and boosting revenue. This led to additional processes and systems being implemented to ensure the customer experience became a priority for everyone. Our leadership team held everyone accountable by modeling the standard we expected and providing coaching support to get everyone to where we collectively needed to be for sustainable success. It sounds great, right? What I had to learn was that not everyone is always compliant or understands the vision set before them, and our priorities are often at odds with each other.

One employee, whom we will call Joe, had a different agenda, as shown by his actions. In our check-ins, we would discuss his opportunities for improvement and success stories, and chart

A RISING GENERATION: THE FUTURE OF LEAD... 137

an agreed-upon path forward to ensure he was growing both as an employee and a human being. We would share learnings from external scenarios, life, work, and family with each other as our partnership with each other grew. However, Joe's behavior did not meet the standard we had set. Based solely on Joe's actions and choices, I had to terminate his employment. This decision was not one I arrived at easily or quickly. I assessed my contribution, or lack thereof, to his under-commitment and sub-par performance before any action steps were taken.

When I arrived at the decision to relieve Joe of his employment, he was fully aware of his actions and took complete ownership of that choice. Surprisingly, in a moment that could have been perceived as awkward or uneasy, there was a sense of peace in the room. So much so that Joe asked me a question I will never forget. He asked me, "How did you become the type of leader you are?" I was taken aback and asked him a bit, wondering why he wanted to know. I wasn't defensive, but rather curious, because at this moment, this question was what I was being asked. Joe responded to me something along the lines of "although I will no longer work for this company, I feel equipped to handle what I am truly good at and committed to, I feel like I have been changed during this experience here, and I've worked for many companies but never experienced this before."

I simply told him that God is the center of my life, and he has changed my perspective on so many things while also giving me the confidence to try new things. After I told him this, he asked me if he could also have God be the center of his life. So, we prayed for his salvation, and he received Jesus into his heart that day. We fell out of contact shortly thereafter, but I learned something from that situation. Joe had identified something transformational in me, and he wanted it in his life. That situation could have ended a million different ways, but it showed me that as leaders, we truly can influence people in ways that we may never see, but our impact can extend far beyond the sphere of a workplace, or team, or family, or whatever you want to use to fill in the blank.

The second story includes my wife and happened during my tenure at an entertainment company. During my time there, I served as a manager, overseeing a team of 500+ people. I didn't have the opportunity to connect with everyone there personally, so my influence often came through developing others and the moments I spoke in front of the entire group. One day, a female we will call Jacky approached me about some personal challenges outside of work that were impacting her performance. I asked whether she had this conversation with her manager and, through discovery, found that the manager dismissed her concern as minimal and chose to prioritize what they believed were higher-priority items. It turns out this woman was suicidal and needed support.

We communicated with human resources, and she was provided the resources she needed to assist her during that challenging moment in her life. I continued to monitor her and her manager from that point forward and made it a point of emphasis for those involved to be mindful but continue to lead appropriately. During that time, Jacky and I would have conversations that left her empowered to navigate challenges both inside and outside the workplace. I communicated with her manager to address her holistically and coach her accordingly. As time went on, Jacky continued to work until one day, she found me walking towards our place of employment. She was in distress and felt as though her only solution would be to take her life.

Against my initial judgment to speak with HR again on her behalf, I redirected her to an older woman who might be able to offer her additional support and insight during this transitional period of her life. That woman happened to be my wife. Jacky was open to having a different perspective. I remained out of their conversations and did not ask for updates, but over the next few weeks, I noticed a change in her behavior. She was more focused, less stressed, and looked as though she was enjoying life again. I recognize there are many factors involved in someone's personal transformation, but witnessing this change in this young woman's life was reassuring for me. Eventually, Jacky approached me, stating her gratitude for her exposure to my wife and the support she had received.

The Why of Transformation

Simon Sinek references a concept called the golden circle in his book Start with Why. The circle consists of three components: what, how, and why. Put simply, many people or organizations are aware of what they do, others are also very clear on how they do it, but the differentiating factor is why they do it.[3] Why not on a surface level, but deeper, more intimate, and more personal? Why represents the purpose, the cause, or the belief behind how and what we do.[4] This principle is timeless and transferable to industries, people groups, activities, you name it. When Simon introduced this concept, he revealed a key to transformational leadership.

Influence and manipulation are comparable in that they can lead others to move towards a cause, but one is self-seeking while the other is selfless. Manipulation is taking advantage of someone or something for your own personal benefit. Influence is the effect your actions have on others that produces change as a lagging indicator. Your efforts today may not yield the results you're looking for tomorrow, but over time, they will have a great impact. When a leader pursues transformation, they must ask themselves why before they begin. Clinton suggests that we lead out of *what we are* not, who we are.[4] The who references our title or position, but the what refers to our character.[1]

Transformational leaders have a why that underlies their actions. They are grounded in their conviction to support others and are acquainted with failure. Lorrits acknowledges the dangers of following a leader who has never failed.[2] If a person has never failed, why would they have a need for transformation? Failure provides leaders with the perspective to learn and the humility to embrace. Without the value failure imparts, leaders are left in a state where arrogance can lead to toxic leadership. I understand; nobody wants to fail at anything, but a transformational leader is not only concerned with the moment but also with the future, recognizing that failure is a springboard to learning and the backdoor to success.

Are You the Next Transformational Leader?

Throughout history, leaders have undergone great personal transformations. These leaders have been defined by their grit, selfless mindsets, and commitment to overcoming adversity despite the circumstances. By examining their journeys, we identified a common thread. True transformation begins within. The individuals we explored did not simply respond to their circumstances; they redefined them. These leaders leveraged their situations as opportunities for impact.

The question now shifts to you. Are you ready to embrace your own transformational journey? Becoming a transformational leader requires humility, vision, willingness to fail, and the ability to navigate risk. It means leading with conviction and advancing regardless of the opposition you're facing. It involves modeling the way by not settling for the status quo or minimizing your opportunity through a lack of discipline.

A RISING GENERATION: THE FUTURE OF LEAD... 141

Leadership is, and will no longer be, solely based on a person's title or position, but on their ability to influence, listen, learn, and remain agile as times change. This road is not for everyone, which is why, at times, it can feel lonely and desolate, but it is a rewarding path to chart. The world needs leaders like you who are willing to get their hands dirty, aren't concerned about position or applause, but truly see the value in others with a desire to help them maximize it. Are you ready to rise to the challenge of becoming the transformational leader your home, your community, and the world need? The choice is yours. The time is ***NOW!***

Don't Just Read. RISE

This book began as a study on transformational leadership, but its purpose is far greater; it's an invitation to live transformed. You are now part of a rising generation, not defined by age but by awareness, courage, and conviction. The world doesn't need another title. It needs another torchbearer.

The Call To Reflect

The next generation must be taught to pause before they perform and to lead from identity, not insecurity. Schools, organizations, and families must cultivate environments that normalize reflection, not reaction.

The Power To Inspire

Young leaders need stories that spark belief. Our responsibility as mentors, teachers, and parents is to model what's possible even when it's hard. When we share our journey holistically, we remind them that leadership is attainable and authentic.

The Responsibility to Serve

The next generation must be shown that leadership is not about the spotlight but stewardship. By teaching the joy of serving others, in small acts or systemic change, we prepare them to build communities that thrive on compassion, not competition.

The Opportunity to Elevate

Our greatest legacy will not be the systems we built or the titles we held, but the people we empowered. To elevate others is to invest in futures we may never see and to plant seeds that will provide shade for generations to come.

---

1. The Holy Bible, New King James Version. (1982). Thomas, Nelson, Inc.

2. Loritts, C.W. (2009). Leadership as an Identity. Moody Publishers.

3. Sinek, S. (2011). Start With Why. Penguin Group.

4. Clinton, J.R. (2012). The Making of a Leader 2nd edition: Recognizing the lessons and stages of leadership development. Tyndale House Publishers, Inc.

Appendix

Ailey, A. (1995). REVELATIONS. The Autobiography of Alvin Ailey. Carol Publishing Group.

Alice Coachman (n.d.). Biography.

Allender, D.B. (2006). Leading With a Limp. Waterbrook Press.

Amy Essington, "Alice Marie Coachman (1923-2014)," Blackpast.org, March 8, 2009, https://www.blackpast.org/african-american-history/coachman-alice-marie-1923/

Avolio, B.J., & Gibbons, T.C. (1988). Developing transformational leaders: A life span approach. Jossey-Bass.

Barna, G. (2018). The Power of Vision 3rd edition. Baker Books.

Bass, B.M., & Riggio, R.E. (2014). Transformational Leadership 2nd edition. Routledge.

Black History Month Moment - Ron Martin presents Max Robinson - YouTube (martin, 2015).

Boyd, H. (2014). Alice Coachman, an immortal Olympian. New York Amsterdam News.

Brody, R. (2016). Hidden Figures is a subtle and powerful work of counter history. The New Yorker.

Brown, B. (2018). Dare to Lead. Random House.

Brown, L.C. (2023). What Makes You Come Alive. Broadleaf Books.

Burns, J.M. (2003). Transforming Leadership. Grove Press.

Carter, S.L. (2018). Invisible. Macmillan Publishing Group.

Canton, J. (2015). Future Smart: Managing the Game-Changing Trends That Will Transform Your World. Da Capo Press.

Chand, S.R. (2015). Leadership Pain: The Classroom for Growth. Thomas Nelson, Inc.

Cloud, H. (2020). Boundaries for Leaders. HarperCollins Publishers.

Clinton, J.R. (2012). The Making of a Leader 2nd edition: Recognizing the lessons and stages of leadership development. Tyndale House Publishers, Inc.

Covey, S. R. (1990). The 7 Habits of Highly Effective People. Irving Perkins Associates.

Cuniberti, B. (1988). Max Robinson's Silent Struggle With Aids. Los Angeles Times. Los Angeles Times (latimes.com)

Dixon-Fyle, S., Hunt, V, Huber, C., Martinez Marquez, M. del M., Prince, S., & Thomas, A. (2023). Diversity Matters Even More: The Case For Holistic Impact. https://www.mckinsey.com/featured-insights/diversity-and-inclusion/diversity-matters-even-more-the-case-for-holistic-impact

Dunning, J. (1998). Alvin Ailey A Life In Dance. Da Capo Press.

Fluker, W.E. (2023). The Unfinished Search for Common Ground. Orbis Books.

Gallo, C. (2014). Talk Like Ted: The 9 Public-Speaking Secrets of the World's Top Minds. St. Martins Griffin.

Goodwin, D.K. (2018). Leadership in Turbulent Times. Simon & Schuster.

Gourani, S. (2024). Why Discipline Outshines Motivation For Effective Leadership. Forbes Magazine.

Hendricks, G. (2009). The Big Leap. HarperCollins Publishers.

Hopson, C. (2021). A Pair of Wings. Jet Black Press.

Johnson, C.E. (2018). Meeting the Ethical Challenges of Leadership: Casting Light or Shadow 7th edition. SAGE Publications, Inc.

Johnson, C.E., & Hackman, M.Z. (2018). Leadership. A Communication Perspective 7th Edition. Waveland Press, Inc.

Kotter, J.P. (1996). Leading Change. Harvard Business Review Press.

Kouzes, J.M., & Posner, B.Z. (2010). The Truth About Leadership. John Wiley & Sons, Inc.

Kouzes, J.M., & Posner, B.Z. (2011). Credibility: How leaders gain and lose it why people demand it. John Wiley & Sons, Inc.

Kouzes, J.M., & Posner, B.Z. (2017). The Leadership Challenge 6th edition. John Wiley & Sons, Inc.

Li, Y. & Greenwald, M.S. (2021). A Lifelong Fight for Social Justice. Fordham University Press.

Loritts, C.W. (2009). Leadership as an Identity. Moody Publishers.

Marvelous Metamorphosis (n.d.). Natural History Museums of Los Angeles County. https://nhmlac.org/marvelous-metamorphosis

Max Robinson, TV News Anchor born - African American Registry (aaregistry.org)

Maxwell, J.C. (2011). The 5 Levels of Leadership. Hachette Book Group.

Mayberry, M. (2024). The Transformational Leader: How the world's best leaders build teams, inspire action, and achieve lasting success. John Wiley & Sons, Inc.

Merriam-Webster. (n.d.). Metamorphosis. In *Merriam-Webster.com dictionary*. Retrieved from https://www.merriam-webster.com/dictionary/metamorphosis

McIntosh, G.L., & Rima, S.D. (2008). Overcoming the Dark Side of Leadership. Baker Books.

Munroe, M. (2005). The Spirit of Leadership. Munroe Group of Companies LTD.

NASA, *Beginners Guide to Aeronautics*, "Four Forces," accessed November 3, 2025, https://www1.grc.nasa.gov/beginners-guide-to-aeronautics/four-forces.

Nick Saban. (2024, Oct 5). On being a 'Transformational Leader' + Cal film room breakdown | College GameDay [Video]. YouTube. https://youtu.be/OJqtnawj7fA?si=ni5yGk-C1ahemHjT

Northouse, P.G. (2021). Leadership Theory & Practice 9th edition. SAGE Publications, Inc.

Parks, G. (1912). Voices in the Mirror an Autobiography. Bantam Doubleday Dell Publishing Group, Inc.

Parks, G. (1966). A Choice of Weapons. Harper & Row.

Plantz, C. (2001). The Life of Bessie Coleman: First African American Woman Pilot. Enslow Publishers, Inc.

Ranger, A. (2023). 5 Stages To Improve Your Photography / A Professional Guide. https://www.alanranger.com/

Sinek, S. (2011). Start With Why. Penguin Group.

Sinek, S. (2024, Jan). Leadership is a Team Sport: [Video] Simon Sinek

Sosik, J.J., & Jung, D. (2018). Full Range Leadership Development. Routledge.

Thurman, H. (1979). With Head and Heart. A Harvest Book Harcourt Brace & Company.

The Holy Bible, New King James Version. (1982). Thomas, Nelson, Inc.

William C. Rhoden, "Good Things Happening for One Who Decided to Wait," *The New York Times*, April 27, 1995

What is my Purpose: Google. (2024). Google Trends. Retrieved [Nov 11, 2024], from https://trends.google.com/trends/explore

White Rose Community TV. (2015, Feb 12). Black History Month Moment - Ron Martin presents Max Robinson: [Video] Max Robinson

Zaleznik, A. (2004). Manager and Leaders: Are They Different? Harvard Business Review.

www.ingramcontent.com/pod-product-compliance
Lightning Source LLC
Chambersburg PA
CBHW052031030426
42337CB00027B/4955